D1824271

Liz Kilbey

Sue Mohamed Sagrario Salaberri Carmen F. Santás

Galaxy

1

Activity
Book

MACMILLAN

Planet Landing

Welcome to the Planet

1 <u>Underline</u> a name and (circle) a country in each sentence.

1 I'm Sue. I'm from England – I'm English.

2 I'm Jenny. I'm from Canada – I'm Canadian.

2 Match the questions to the answers.

1	What's your name?	a	Green.
2	Where are you from?	b	Jo.
3	What's your favourite colour?	c	England.

3 Colour in the rainbow and label the colours.

> red   orange   yellow   green
> blue   indigo   violet

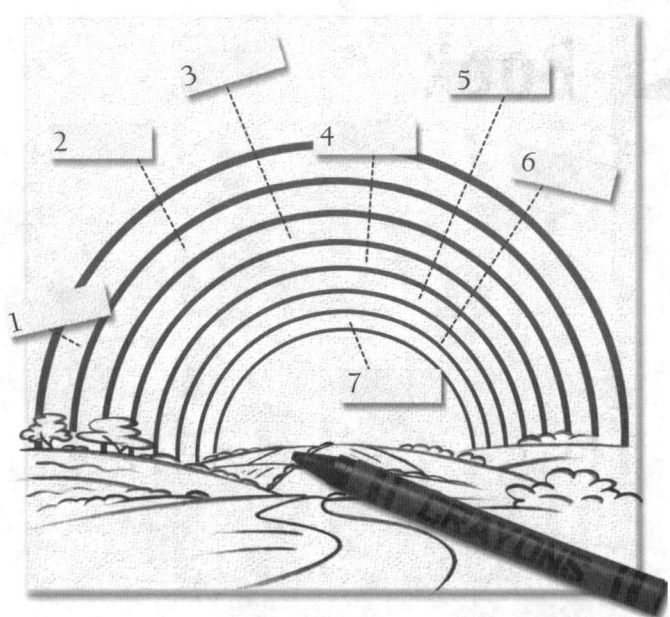

4 Colour the shirts.

zero is green   six is white
one is purple   seven is black
two is yellow   eight is blue
three is brown   nine is pink
four is red   ten is your
five is orange   favourite colour!

2

Steady Steady Steady Steady Steady Steady

1 **Complete the dialogue.**

a: Hi, _I'm Sarah._ What's _____
_____ ?

b: My _____ Jonathan.
_____ are you _____ ?

a: I'm _____ Ireland. _____
Irish. Where _____
_____ from?

b: _____ from England.

2 **Now write about Jonathan.**

Hi, I'm Jonathan. _____
_____
_____

Now write about Sarah.

Hi, I'm Sarah. _____
_____
_____

3 **Find the names of six colours in the
wordsearch. Write the colours and fill the
circles with the correct colour.**

```
w  n  l  l  y  o  e  b
y  e  w  b  e  d  r  l
e  g  e  o  w  k  u  e
l  r  r  w  r  n  k  u
l  b  o  e  i  b  c  l
o  k  d  s  e  u  a  b
w  c  a  r  g  n  l  t
b  l  s  a  c  m  b  s
```

( ) ( )

_____red_____   _____

( ) ( )

_____   _____

( ) ( )

_____   _____

1a Make questions from the words.

1 name / What's / your / ?

_____

2 from / are / Where / you / ?

_____

3 colour / your / favourite / What's / ?

_____

1b Now match the questions with these answers.

a My favourite colour is orange. ☐

b Hi, I'm David. ☐

c I'm from Planet Orb. ☐

2 Complete the dialogue.

DANIEL: Hello, I'm Daniel.

YOU: Hi, _____.

DANIEL: I'm from Planet Orb. Where are you from?

YOU: I'm _____.

What's _____

_____?

DANIEL: Black. _____

_____ colour?

YOU: _____.

3a Choose the correct word to fill each gap.

red + yellow = orange

one + two = three

1 blue + _____ = green

four + _____ = _____

2 _____ + _____ = purple

four + _____ = _____

3 red + _____ = pink

_____ + seven = _____

3b Colour the numbers!

1	2	3	4

5	6	7	8

Welcome to the spaceship

Ready   Ready   Ready   Ready   Ready   Ready

1   **Find the names of the objects and complete the puzzle.**

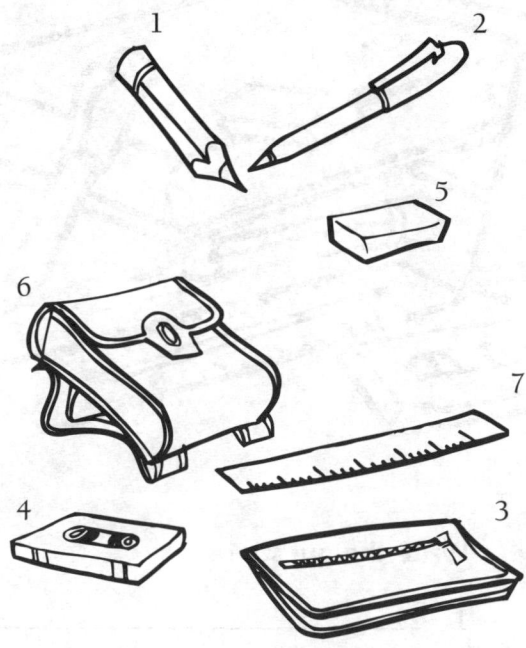

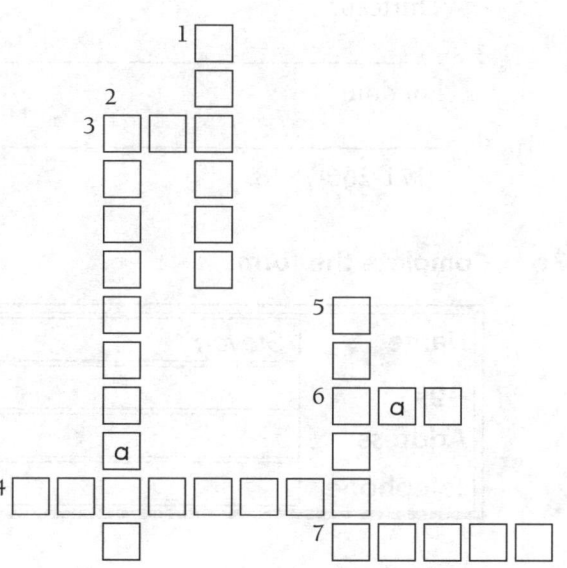

2   **Make sentences.**

have / you / got / a / pencil / ?

<u>Have you got a pencil?</u>

1   he / hasn't / got / a / ruler / .

2   she's / got / a / pen / .

3   has / he / got / a / rubber / ?

4   has / she / got / a / bag / ?

5   I / haven't / got / a / pen / .

6   she / hasn't / got / a / cassette / .

3   **Choose the correct words for each picture.**

boy	dark	fair	girl	short	tall

Mandy   Steven

_____   _____

_____   _____

Steady Steady Steady Steady Steady Steady

1 **Look at the picture and label the objects.**

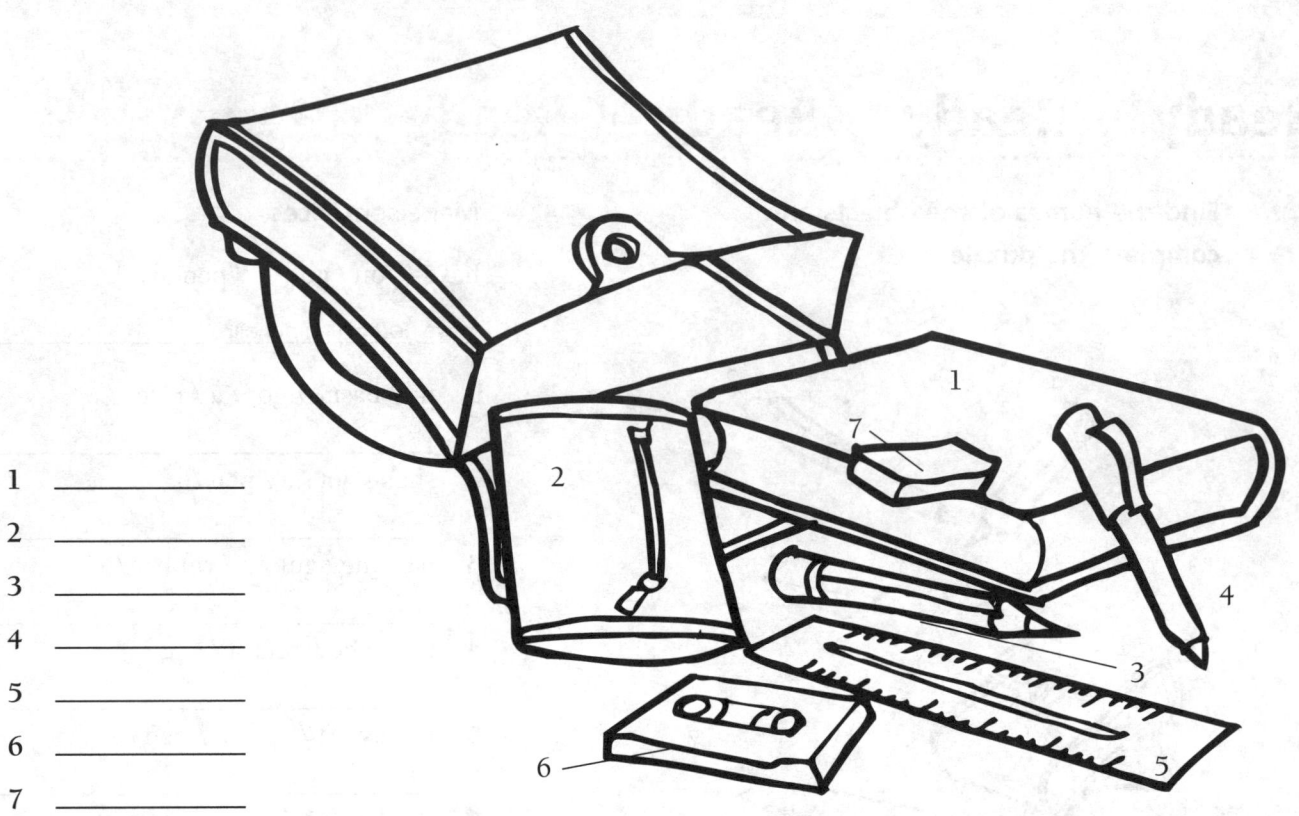

1 _____

2 _____

3 _____

4 _____

5 _____

6 _____

7 _____

2 **Look in your bag. Answer the questions.**

1 Have you got a pencil-case?

_____

2 Have you got a pen?

_____

3 Have you got a ruler?

_____

4 Have you got a rubber?

_____

5 Have you got a cassette?

_____

6 Have you got a book?

_____

7 Have you got a pencil?

_____

8 Have you got a sandwich?

_____

3a **Write the questions.**

1 _____?

Steven.

2 _____?

Thirteen.

3 _____?

London.

4 _____?

0171-266-7848.

3b **Complete the form.**

Name	Steven
Age	
Address	
Telephone	

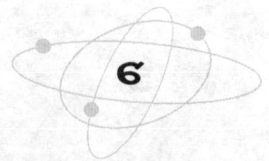

Go Go Go Go Go Go Go Go Go Go Go Go Go

1a **Look at the passwords. Match with the pictures.**

1 GISHFASADU11
   girl, short, fair, Sarah, 11

2 BOTADAJALO12
   _____

3 BOTAFALURO11
   _____

4 GITADACLPA12
   _____

James, 12, London   Sarah, 11, Dublin

Claire, 12, Paris   Luigi, 11, Rome

1b **Who am I? Write the correct names.**

1 I'm Italian.
   _____

2 I'm Irish.
   _____

3 I'm English.
   _____

4 I'm French.
   _____

2 **Write sentences about James, Sarah, Claire and Luigi.**

James has got a bag and a book.

Sarah _____

Claire _____

Luigi _____

3 **Write the words in the puzzle.**

Across

1

4

5

Down

1

2

3

7

Planet People

1a

Hi, I'm Amy. I'm from Canada.

Hi! We're Bill and Claire. We're from England.

Hello. I'm Roberto. I'm from Spain.

Hi, I'm Lisa. I'm Canadian.

1 Look at the pictures. Choose the correct word to complete each sentence.

> they they're ~~she~~ ~~she's~~ we
> we're he he's it she she's

1 Is Amy English? No, <u>she</u> isn't. <u>She's</u> Canadian.

2 Are Bill and Claire Spanish? No, _____ aren't. _____ English.

3 Is Lisa English? No, _____ isn't. _____ Canadian.

4 Is Roberto English? No, _____ isn't. _____ Spanish.

5 "Lisa, are you and Amy English?"
"No, _____ aren't. _____ Canadian."

6 "Is this your luggage?"
"Yes, _____ is."

2 Fill in your luggage label.

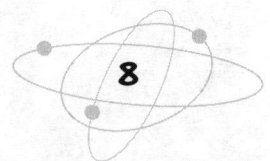
First name ....
Surname ....
Address ....
Telephone number ....

3 Match the questions and answers.

1	Is Bill Spanish?	a	Yes, they are.
2	Are Lisa and Amy English?	b	Holmes.
3	Is Amy Canadian?	c	No, it isn't.
4	Are we friends?	d	No, he isn't.
5	Is this your luggage?	e	Yes, we are.
6	What's your surname?	f	No, they aren't.
7	Are Lisa and Amy Canadian?	g	Yes, she is.

4 Write the words in the correct order!

1  is friend. my This's

This is my friend. _____

2 YOU please your? Can spell surname

_____

3 They English aren't

_____

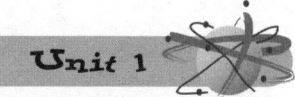

Steady Steady Steady Steady Steady Steady

1a Look at the lost luggage form. Write the missing words in the correct places.

Amy   24 Station Road, Cambridge
01223 45896   Holmes

Telephone number ....
Surname ....
First name ....
Address ....
....

1b Complete the dialogue.

MAN: Now, what's _____
_____ , please?

AMY: Amy Holmes.

MAN: Can you _____ your
_____ , please?

AMY: H.O.L.M.E.S.

MAN: Thank you. And _____
your _____?

AMY: 24 Station Road, Cambridge.

MAN: And what's your _____
_____?

AMY: 01223 45896.

2 Complete the questions and answers.

1   _____ Lisa your friend?
Yes, she is.

2   _____ this your luggage?
No, it _____.

3   _____ we friends?
Yes, _____ are.

4   _____ Claire Spanish? No, she
_____. _____ English.

5   _____ Lisa and Amy
friends?
Yes, _____ _____.

6   _____ you Spanish?
Yes, I _____.

7   _____ Bill English?
Yes, _____ is.

8   _____ Lisa and Amy
Canadian?
Yes, _____ _____.

3 Find six sentences! Add CAPITAL LETTERS, ????question marks???? and .....full stops...... .

heisenglishwhat'syouraddressweareenglishnicetomeetyouI'mnotenglishcanyouspellyoursurnameplease

He is English. _____
1   _____
2   _____
3   _____
4   _____
5   _____

Go Go Go Go Go Go Go Go Go Go Go Go Go Go

1a **Look at this. Fill in the gaps.**

LOST LUGGAGE	
	Holmes
First name	Amy
	24 Station Road, Cambridge
	01223 45896

1b **Write the dialogue.**

MAN: _____?

AMY: Amy Holmes _____

MAN: _____?

AMY: H.O.L.M.E.S. _____

MAN: _____?

AMY: _____

MAN: _____?

AMY: _____

1c **Complete the questions and answer them about you!**

1   What's _____ address?

   _____

2   _____ _____ telephone number?

   _____

3   _____ _____ surname?

   _____

2a **Read the passage and answer the questions.**

Lisa and Amy are friends. They're Canadian. They're students at a school in Cambridge. Roberto is Spanish and he's also in Cambridge. Bill and Claire are English. They're teachers at the school.

1   Is Lisa a student?   Yes, she is.

2   Is Bill a student?

   _____

3   Where are Lisa and Amy?

   _____

4   Is Roberto in Spain?

   _____

5   Where are Bill and Claire?

   _____

2b **Look at pages 8 and 9 in your Student's Book. Write about Patrick.**

_____

_____

_____

_____

3 **Write sentences about yourself and your friends and your family.**

Useful words			
mother	father	brother	sister

I'm _____. I'm from _____

My address is

_____

My friends are _____

_____

My father is _____

_____

_____

Planet People

1b

1 Find twelve adjectives!

friendlyunhappyromanticserious
funhappyunromantic
kindgenerousmeanunkindfununfriendly

kind _____   _____

_____   _____

_____   _____

_____   _____

_____   _____

_____   _____

2 Find the numbers 1 to 9!

t	o	w	f	I	n	l
o	n	e	h	s	i	x
s	f	i	v	e	n	m
e	i	g	h	v	e	n
a	t	h	r	e	e	n
t	w	t	h	n	u	s
f	o	u	r	e	x	i

3 Choose the correct word to complete each sentence.

are	are	are	am	am	aren't
isn't	aren't	isn't			

I'm not unfriendly, I _am_ friendly.

1 You _____ kind, thank you.

2 He _____ friendly, he is unfriendly.

3 They _____ fun, they aren't serious.

4 She is generous, she _____ mean.

5 I _____ happy. I'm not unhappy.

6 We _____ romantic, we're unromantic!

7 We aren't unfriendly, we _____ friendly.

8 They are unkind, they _____ kind.

4 Write these nouns in the correct column.

mother	father	friends	my dog
teachers	brother	sister	Italy
Eva	Peter	Britain	dogs	

	he	she
	father _____	_____
	_____	_____
	_____	_____
	it	they
	_____	_____
	_____	_____
	_____	_____

11

Steady Steady Steady Steady Steady Steady

1 **Find the numbers 1 to 9!**

> vefi   vesen   inen   wot   ereth
> rouf   xsi   thgie   noe

one _____   _____

_____   _____

_____   _____

_____   _____

_____

2 **Write the telephone numbers.**

1   13685   one three six eight five _____

2   29876   _____

3   89297   _____

4   13498   _____

5   _____   three seven six two one

6   _____   six four five three seven

7   _____   nine two three one eight

3 **Make adjectives!**

1   soregneu   generous _____

2   eman   _____

3   eyinfrld   _____

4   toiramnc   _____

5   yphap   _____

6   nuf   _____

7   soeisru   _____

8   nhupypa   _____

4 **Look at the words and finish the sentences.**

1   unhappy   4   unkind
2   mean   5   unromantic
3   fun   6   unfriendly

Number <u>one</u> is the opposite of <u>happy</u>.

Number <u>two</u> is the opposite of

_____.

Number t __ r __ e is the opposite of

_____.

Number f __ __ __ is the opposite of

_____.

Number __ __ __ __ is the opposite of

_____.

Number __ __ __ is the opposite of

_____.

5 **Fill in the gaps.**

1   I am   I'm _____
2   I am not   _____
3   He is   _____
4   He is not   He isn't
5   _____   She's
6   She is not   _____
7   _____   It's
8   It is not   _____
9   _____   You're
10 You are not   _____
11 We are   _____
12 _____   We aren't
13 _____   They're
14 They are not   _____

12

Go Go Go Go Go Go Go Go Go Go Go Go Go Go

1a Find six adjectives.

```
g e l l c k k b
l f n r i s n n
f s e s t c s w
r o m a n s k i
p f d s a e g e
k r n d m r x s
w i a l o i k d
g e n e r o u s
c n b d f u s z
k d m m f s d j
t l d s t l e e
l y p p a h c g
```

1b Write the adjectives here.

1 friendly
2 _____
3 _____
4 _____
5 _____
6 _____

2a Write sentences.

kind
generous
romantic

1 Sarah is kind. She isn't unkind. She's generous.
   _____

friendly
fun

2 Martin _____
   _____

serious
unhappy

3 Ann and Lee _____
   _____

2b What about you?

I am _____
_____

My friend is _____
_____

We aren't _____
_____

3a Complete the sums with the correct numbers.

one + three = four

1 _____ + six = nine
2 eight − seven = _____
3 six − _____ = two
4 _____ + _____ = nine
5 _____ + _____ = eight
6 _____ − _____ = four
7 _____ + _____ = six
8 _____ − _____ = two

3b Complete the sums and write the answers.

1 ten / two = five

2 twelve / six = _____

3 eight / two = _____

4 three × three = _____
5 one × two = _____
6 two × five = _____

13

B*witched

are a girl band. The four girls in the band are Sinead O'Carroll, Lindsay Armaou, and Edele and Keavy Lynch. They are all very young – but they are mega successful!!

The girls are from Dublin, Ireland. Their songs are fast and happy and there is lots of Irish music and dancing at their concerts. They are all from musical families and they are all brilliant dancers. Edele and Keavy are twin sisters – and their brother Shane is a member of the band Boyzone, so there are three superstars in one family!!! Their songs are: 'C'est La Vie', 'Rollercoaster', 'To you I belong', 'Blame it on the Weatherman', 'Jesse Hold On'.

Another very young and very successful British band is

S Club 7

There are three boys (Paul, Jon and Bradley) and four girls (Tina, Jo, Hannah and Rachel) in the band and their songs 'Bring it all Back' and 'S Club Party' are very big hits. Their music is very popular with young teenagers in Britain and there is lots of dancing on stage from them, too.

Questions
1 Do you know their music?
2 What kind of music do you like?
3 Write about your favourite band.

Planet People

2a

Ready Ready Ready Ready Ready Ready

 1a **Draw the missing hands!**

1   It's ten o'clock.   2   It's quarter to two.

3   It's eleven o'clock.   4   It's half past seven.

5   It's quarter past one.   6   It's half past five.

1b **Choose the correct word to complete each sentence.**

to	half	twelve	half	past
o'clock				

12.00 It's <u>twelve</u> o'clock.

1   6.30 It's _____ past six.

2   2.45 It's quarter _____ three.

3   7.30 It's _____ past seven.

4   5.00 It's five _____.

5   1.15 It's quarter _____ one.

2 **Tick (✓) the correct answers.**

Do you have lunch at night?
Yes, I do. ☐ No, I don't. ✓

1   Do you clean your teeth in the morning?
Yes, I do. ☐ No, I don't. ☐

2   Do you watch TV in the evening?
Yes, I do. ☐ No, I don't. ☐

3   Do you go to bed in the morning?
Yes, I do. ☐ No, I don't. ☐

4   Do you go to school at night?
Yes, I do. ☐ No, I don't. ☐

5   Do you have lunch at midday?
Yes, I do. ☐ No, I don't. ☐

3 **Underline the correct words.**

My friend *gets up / get up* at six o'clock.
1   They *has / have* lunch at one o'clock.
2   We *watch / watches* TV in the evening.
3   She *goes / go* to bed at ten o'clock.
4   I *go / goes* to school at eight o'clock.
5   Rudolph and Vanessa *drinks / drink* blood.
6   My sister and I *have / has* breakfast at eight o'clock.
7   He *brushes / brush* his teeth in the morning.
8   You *play / plays* sport in the afternoon.
9   I *brush / brushes* my teeth at night.
10 We *get up / gets up* at six o'clock.

Steady Steady Steady Steady Steady Steady

1 Write sentences.

John / *get* up / 7 a.m.
John gets up at seven o'clock in the morning.

1   I / *go* to bed / 10.30 p.m.

_____
_____

2   We / *have* dinner / 6 p.m.

_____
_____

3   She / *have* lunch / 12.15 p.m.

_____
_____

4   You / *play* sport / 3.00 p.m.

_____
_____

5   They / *get* up / 7.15 a.m.

_____
_____

6   Sally and I / *have* breakfast / 8.30 a.m.

_____
_____

7   Rudolph and Vanessa / *drink* blood / night

_____
_____

2 Complete the questions.

1   What time <u>do you get up</u>? I get up at 6.30!
2   _____
    _____ you _____ lunch?
    2.15.
3   What _____
    _____?
    We go to bed at 11.
4   _____ time _____
    _____?
    I go to school at nine.

3 Make sentences with words from each box.

I	You	He	She	We	They
My friend		Rudolph and Vanessa			

have	go	<u>play</u>	drink	watch
		get up		

<u>sport</u>	blood	TV	breakfast	lunch
	dinner	to school	to bed	

at	<u>in</u>

the morning	the afternoon
<u>the evening</u>	night	midday
	midnight	

I play sport in the evening.

1   _____
2   _____
3   _____
4   _____
5   _____
6   _____

4 Tick (✓) the correct sentences and ~~Cross out~~ the mistakes.

He gets up at six.   ✓

~~He get up at six.~~

1   a   We has breakfast at eight.

    b   We have breakfast at eight.

2   a   They watches TV in the evening.

    b   They watch TV in the evening.

3   a   John goes to bed at ten.

    b   John go to bed at ten.

4   a   I play sport at the morning.

    b   I play sport in the morning.

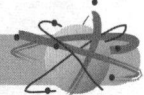

Go Go Go Go Go Go Go Go Go Go Go Go Go

1 **Look at dialogue A and paragraph B. Use the information to fill each gap.**

A

JOHN: <u>What time do you get up?</u>

PAUL: <u>I get up at 7.00 a.m.</u>

JOHN: [1] _____?

PAUL: I go to school at 8.30.

JOHN: [2] _____?

PAUL: We have lunch at 12.

JOHN: [3] _____?

PAUL: I play sport in the afternoon.

JOHN: [4] _____?

PAUL: I watch TV.

JOHN: [5] _____?

PAUL: 9.45.

B

Paul <u>gets up</u> at seven in the morning.

He [1] _____ half past eight.

Paul [2] _____ midday.

Paul [3] _____ the afternoon.

In the evening he [4] _____ .

Paul [5] _____ to bed [6] _____ quarter

[7] _____ ten.

2 **Write questions for the answers.**

1 <u>What time do you go to bed?</u>
   I go to bed at half past ten.

2 _____?
   I play sport at three.

3 _____?
   We have dinner at half past six.

4 _____?
   I watch TV.

5 _____?
   I get up at eight o'clock.

3 **Answer the questions. Write sentences.**

1 What time do you get up?
   _____

2 What time do you go to school?
   _____

3 What time do you have lunch?
   _____

4 What time do you go to bed?
   _____

4 **What do you do on holiday? Write sentences.**

<u>I get up at eleven. I have a big breakfast.</u>
_____
_____
_____
_____

Planet People

2b

1 Look at the family tree. Write the correct names.

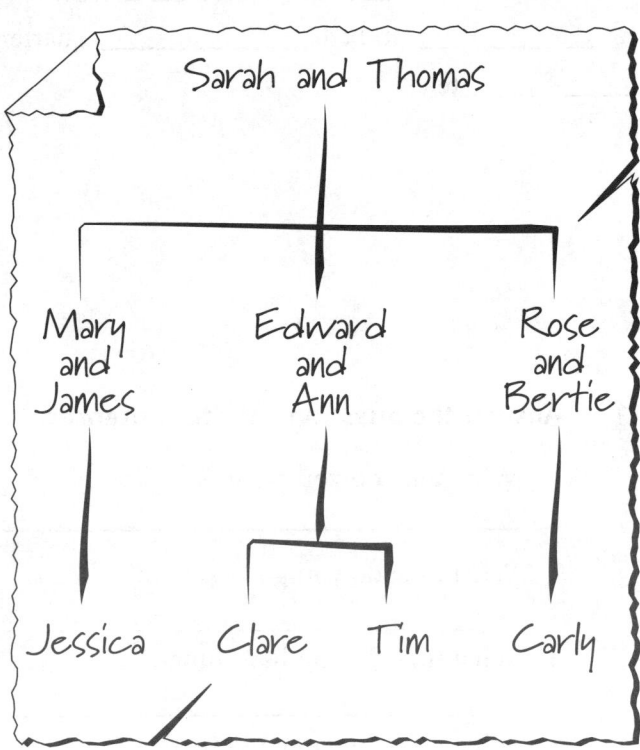

Sarah and Thomas

Mary and James   Edward and Ann   Rose and Bertie

Jessica   Clare   Tim   Carly

Her mother is Mary.
Jessica.

1 Her father is Edward.
_____

2 Their mother is Ann.
_____ and _____

3 Carly is his daughter.
_____

4 His grandmother is Sarah.
_____

5 Her brother is Tim.
_____

2 Choose the correct word to complete each sentence.

their   her   his   your   our

1 (Rose)
<u>Her</u> father is Thomas.

2 (Tim)
_____ sister is Clare.

3 "We are Mary and Rose.
_____ mother is Sarah."

4 (Ann)
_____ son is Tim.

5 (Rose and Bertie)
_____ daughter is Carly.

6 "Mary, is _____ daughter Jessica?"
"Yes, she is."

3 Answer the questions. Choose answers from the box.

Yes, she does. / No, she doesn't.
Yes, I do. / No, I don't.
Yes, they do. / No, they don't.

1 Do you play sport?
_____

2 Do you clean the kitchen?
_____

3 Does your mother cook?
_____

4 Do your mother and father watch TV?
_____

Steady Steady Steady Steady Steady Steady

1 Look at the British Royal Family family tree. Complete the sentences.

Elizabeth and Philip

Charles and Diana | Anne and Mark | Andrew and Sarah | Edward and Sophie

William Harry | Eugenie | Beatrice

Zara Peter

"Our mother is Anne. We are <u>Zara</u> and <u>Peter.</u>"

1 Their sister is Anne.

They are _____,

_____ and _____.

2 Their sons are _____,

_____ and _____.

They are Elizabeth and Philip.

3 "_____ father is Charles.

We _____."

4 Her father is Mark.

She _____

5 _____ Anne.

_____ is Peter.

6 "_____ mother is Diana.

We are _____."

7 "_____ mother is Sarah.

We are _____."

8 "I'm Beatrice and this is Philip."

"Is he _____ father?"

"No! He isn't my father. He's my

_____!"

2a Look at the chart and write sentences.

	play games	play sport	watch TV	read	cook
Jessica	✓	✗	✓	✗	✗
Clare	✓	✗	✓	✗	✗
Tim	✓	✓	✓	✗	✗
Carly	✗	✓	✓	✓	✓
Your name					

Jessica (watch TV / read)

<u>Jessica watches TV. She doesn't read.</u>

1 Tim (cook / sport)

_____

2 Carly (games / sport)

_____

3 Jessica and Clare (cook)

_____

4 Tim and Carly (watch TV)

_____

Now complete the chart for you!

2b Write questions and answers.

Jessica / play games?

<u>Does Jessica play games?</u>   <u>Yes, she does.</u>

1 Clare / play sport

_____?

2 Tim / watch TV

_____?

3 Jessica and Tim / read

_____?

4 Carly / cook

_____?

_____

Go Go Go Go Go Go Go Go Go Go Go Go Go Go

1 **Complete the questions and answers.**

1 (she / sport) <u>Does she play sport?</u>
No, <u>she doesn't.</u>

2 (they / TV) _____?
Yes, _____

3 (he / read) _____?
Yes, _____

4 (you / cook) _____?
No, _____

5 (she / clean the kitchen)

_____?

Yes, _____

6 (you / games) _____?
Yes, _____

2a **Read the passage and fill each gap with one word.**

Jo, Les and Dominic [1] <u>live</u> in Birmingham.
Jo is Dominic's mother. Les is his father. James
is Jo's father and Mary is Jo's mother. They live
[2] _____ Manchester. Lianne is
Dominic's sister. She [3] _____ in
London.

Dominic and Lianne don't [4] _____
games in the evening. [5] _____ play
sport and watch TV. They [6] _____
read and they [7] _____ cook. Jo
doesn't [8] _____ games. She
[9] _____ sport and she
[10] _____ TV. She
[11] _____ read, but [12] _____
cooks. Les [13] _____ play games.
[14] _____ plays sport and
[15] _____ TV. He [16] _____
read and [17] _____ doesn't cook.

2b **Complete the chart.**

	play games	play sport	watch TV	read	cook
Dominic	✓				
Lianne					
Jo					
Les					

2c **Draw the family tree.**

2d **Answer the questions.**

1 Who is Dominic's grandfather?

_____

2 Who is Dominic's grandmother?

_____

3 Who live in Birmingham?

_____

4 Who live in Manchester?

_____

5 Who lives in London?

_____

3 **Now you! Write about your family
(mother, father, grandmother, grandfather,
sister, brother). Where do they live? What
do they do?**

_____

_____

_____

_____

_____

SLEEP

1 Do you like bedtime? What time do you go to bed? Are you tired at bedtime? Do you read in bed, or listen to music ... or do you just fall asleep? How many hours do you sleep? What happens when you sleep?

2 When you sleep, your body temperature drops ... and your weight drops, too!

3 People of different ages need different amounts of sleep – and they also get tired at different times. A new baby has about 16 hours sleep every 24 hours (that's lots of short sleeps, not one long one!). Your parents need about eight hours sleep, but your grandparents probably need less.

4 You probably need about nine hours sleep every night – but do you get it? Do you go to sleep when you go to bed? Are you awake at bedtime and tired in the morning? Do your parents get tired before you do?

5 A lot of teenagers (and their parents!) have this problem. Some scientists say that young people actually have different sleep patterns, so maybe it's not all those parties and TV programmes!

So, when you get up tomorrow morning, remember – teenagers all over the world feel awful, too!

Questions

1 How many hours sleep do you have?

2 How many hours sleep do you need?!

21

Planet Nature

3a

1a **Find ten animals. Write the names.**

```
c  b  i  r  d  a  y  t  r
h  e  s  h  e  e  p  n  f
c  a  b  m  k  k  y  e  i
i  r  d  n  e  a  r  p  s
r  h  o  p  s  n  h  r  h
t  m  b  c  o  s  n  e  c
s  m  o  n  o  d  o  n  o
o  i  l  f  i  d  h  o  d
t  n  a  h  p  e  i  i  h
d  t  n  a  h  p  e  l  e
e  a  r  b  h  s  e  p  e
```

1 bird _____   6 _____
2 _____   7 _____
3 _____   8 _____
4 _____   9 _____
5 _____   10 _____

1b *a* or *an*? **Write the animals in the correct column.**

a	an
a bird	

2 **Look at the picture and write sentences.**

There are some monkeys. _____

1 _____
2 _____
3 _____
4 _____
5 _____
6 _____
7 _____
8 _____

3 **Look at page 21 in the Student's Book. Tick (✓) the correct sentences. Cross out the wrong sentences.**

~~Amazon parrots live in China.~~

1 Giant pandas eat bamboo. ✓
2 Indian rhinos eat animals.
3 Amazon parrots eat fruit and seeds.
4 Indian rhinos live in forests.
5 Giant pandas live in Spain.
6 There are lots of giant pandas in the world.

Steady   Steady   Steady   Steady   Steady   Steady

1   **What is it?**

1   2   3   4   5   6

7   8   9   10

1   It's a monkey.   6   _____

2   _____   7   _____

3   _____   8   _____

4   _____   9   _____

5   _____   10   _____

2   **Tick (✓) the correct sentences. Rewrite the wrong sentences.**

There are some birds.   ✓

_____

There's a elephant.   ✗
There's an elephant.

1   There are some monkey.   ☐

_____

2   There are some sheep.   ☐

_____

3   There's a snake.   ☐

_____

4   There are a bear.   ☐

_____

5   There are some lions.   ☐

_____

6   There's some crocodiles.   ☐

_____

3   **Read the passage and answer the questions.**

Some animals in Britain are in danger. A lot of small animals live in the forests but there are not a lot of forests left. Some people kill animals and birds to eat, or for sport. There are zoos, of course, and the animals there are not in danger, but are they happy?

1   Are there any small animals in British forests these days?

Yes, there are.

2   Are there many forests in Britain these days?

_____

3   Do people in Britain kill animals and birds for sport?

_____

4   Are there any zoos in Britain?

_____

5   Are zoo animals happy? What do you think?

_____

1 **What are they?**

1

richostkesna

a snake and an ostrich

2

eleplimonhantkeyon

_____ ,

_____ and _____

3

snabifielebearhantkeshrd

_____

4

shebesncrocodileeparake

_____

2 **Look at the pictures of animals in danger.
Write sentences.**

> elephant   falcon   parrot   seal
> tiger   tortoise   whale

There's an elephant. _____

1 _____

2 _____

3 _____

4 _____

5 _____

6 _____

3a **Read the text and answer the questions.**

Elephants are in danger because people kill
them for their tusks. Some people kill falcons
for sport. Other birds are in danger, too – for
example, parrots. People don't kill parrots, but
they sell them in other countries as pets.
Parrots don't like cold countries, and a lot of
them die.

1 Why do people kill elephants?

_____

2 Why are falcons in danger?

_____

3 What happens to parrots?

_____

3b **Choose two of the animals in danger. Why
are they in danger? Use the words in the
box to help you.**

> fur   meat   pets   shell   skin
> sport   tusks

_____

_____

_____

Planet Nature

3b

1a   **Write the correct names for the food.**

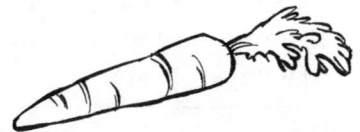  

1 <u>carrot</u>   2 _____   3 _____

  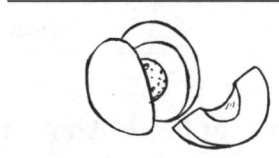

4 _____   5 _____   6 _____

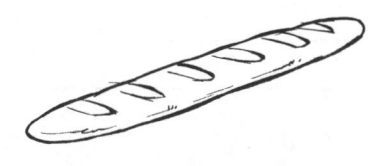 

7 _____   8 _____

1b   **Use these words to make sentences about the pictures. Start each sentence with *There*.**

is	are	a	an	some

1 There <u>is a carrot.</u> _____
2 There _____
3 There _____
4 There _____
5 There _____
6 There _____
7 There _____
8 There _____

2   **Choose the correct word to fill each gap.**

~~any~~	any	any	any	are	are
aren't	~~is~~	is	is	isn't	some

A: <u>Is</u> there <u>any</u> milk?

B: No, there _____ .

A: And bread – _____ there _____ bread?

B: Yes, there _____ .

A: Tomatoes?

B: Yes, there _____ _____ tomatoes.

A: Good. _____ there _____ carrots?

B: Ummm – no, there _____ .
Oh, and there aren't _____ potatoes.

Steady Steady Steady Steady Steady Steady

1 **Complete the table.**

singular	plural
bread	✗
tomato	tomatoes
milk	
potato	
cheese	
	carrots
rice	
oil	
	peaches

2a **What's for lunch? Look at the meals. Complete the sentences.**

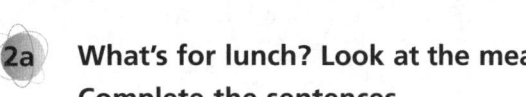

1 Some meat and some potatoes.

2 _____

3 _____

4 _____

2b **Look at the four meals again. Make sentences.**

There	is isn't are aren't	a an some any	bread butter orange carrots tomato cheese meat milk cake potatoes fish

1 There is some meat and there are some potatoes.

2 _____
   _____

3 _____
   _____

4 _____
   _____

3 **You're hungry! Ask six questions. Choose words from the box.**

apples biscuits bread cake
cheese ham milk orange juice
pasta

Are there any apples?

1 _____
2 _____
3 _____
4 _____
5 _____
6 _____

26

Go Go Go Go Go Go Go Go Go Go Go Go Go Go

1a Look at the picture clues and write the words in the correct places in the puzzle. Use *a*, *an* or *some*.

Across

1   2

4   5

Down

1   2

3

1b Each sentence has one mistake. Underline the mistake and correct it.

1 There <u>are</u> some bread.   is _____

2 There is an oil. _____

3 There are a peaches. _____

4 There are some milk. _____

5 There is some carrots. _____

6 There is a potatoes. _____

7 There is some tomato. _____

8 There is a rice. _____

2 Write questions and answers.

Is there any milk? _____

No, there isn't. _____

1 _____
_____?
_____

2 _____
_____?
_____

3 _____
_____?
_____

4 _____
_____?
_____

5 _____
_____?
_____

6 _____
_____?
_____

7 _____
_____?
_____

27

What is it?

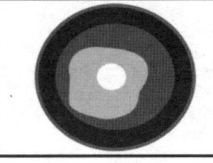

It's an egg on a plate.

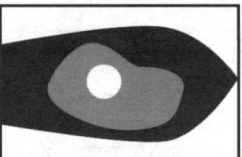

It's an egg in a boat.

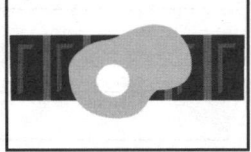

It's an egg on a wall.

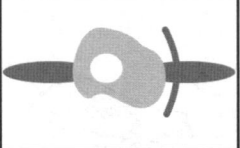

It's an egg on a bicycle.

It's a ghost.

It's a ghost with a friend.

It's a ghost with something in its eye.

What's got eleven heads and twenty two legs?

A football team.

What's black and white and has got 16 wheels?

A zebra on roller skates.

What's got fifty legs?

Half a centipede.

What looks like half an apple?

The other half.

What's black and white and very dangerous?

Ice cream with sharks in it.

What's pink and black and very dangerous?

Strawberry ice cream with sharks in it.

Planet Weather

4a

1 Look at the weather map and complete each sentence.

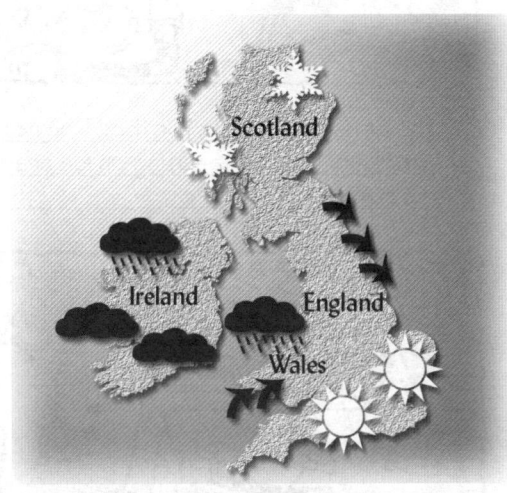

| cloudy   rainy   snowy   sunny |
| windy |

1 It's _____ in Scotland.

2 It's _____ and
  _____ in England.

3 It's _____ and
  _____ in Ireland.

4 It's _____ and
  _____ in Wales.

2 Underline the correct word in each sentence.

1 It's *sun* / *sunny*.

2 There's a lot of *rain* / *rainy*.

3 It's *foggy* / *fog* today.

4 There's some *snow* / *snowy*.

5 *It's* / *There's* foggy.

6 *It's* / *There's* windy.

3 Write the sentences.

1 _____

2 _____

3 _____

4 _____

4 Choose the correct word to fill each gap.

| cooking   playing   reading |
| watching   are   is   because |

Rob isn't [1] _____ football

[2] _____ it's raining. He's

[3] _____ TV. His sister Ann

[4] _____ [5] _____ a book.

Their mother and father [6] _____

[7] _____ dinner.

5 Answer the questions.

| Yes, it is.   Yes, I am. |
| No, it isn't.   No, I'm not. |

1 Are you listening to music now?

  _____

2 Is it raining now?

  _____

3 Are you sleeping now?

  _____

29

1 **Rewrite each sentence.**

1   It's rainy.
   <u>There's a lot of rain.</u>

2   It's cloudy.
   _____

3   _____
   There's a lot of snow.

4   _____
   There's a lot of fog.

5   It's windy.
   _____

6   _____
   There's a lot of sun.

2 **Make sentences using *but, and* or *because*.**

1	It's sunny		it's cold.
2	It's raining	but	it's windy.
3	Rainforests are hot	because and	they're near the equator.
4	It's snowing		it isn't cold.
5	It's cloudy		the sun is shining.

3 **Read the passage and write the verbs (in brackets) in their correct form.**

Paul and Andrew are at school. It's 11.30 and they [1] _____ _____ (study) Maths. The teacher [2] _____ _____ (talk) and [3] _____ _____ (write) on the blackboard. Paul [4] _____ _____ (write). Andrew [5] _____ _____ (not write). He [6] _____ _____ (sleep).

4 **Look at the pictures and write sentences.**

1   <u>The boys are playing football. The man is watching. The girl is eating an ice cream. It's sunny.</u>

2   _____
   _____
   _____
   _____

3   _____
   _____
   _____
   _____

Go Go Go Go Go Go Go Go Go Go Go Go Go Go Go

1 **Tick (✓) the correct sentences. Rewrite the wrong sentences.**

It's sun in the summer. ☒

It's sunny in summer.

1 It's foggy. ✓

_____

2 There's a lot of rainy. ☐

_____

3 There's a lot of cloud. ☐

_____

4 It's windy in autumn. ☐

_____

5 There's sunny today. ☐

_____

6 It's snow in winter. ☐

_____

2 **Sam likes the summer and Hayley likes the winter. Read what they say and answer the questions.**

> I like the summer because we go on holiday to the seaside. It's hot and sunny and we swim everyday. Why do you like the winter?

> Because in the winter we stay at home and watch TV and play music! We don't play a lot of sport in winter – I don't like sport! And Christmas is great!

1 Which season do you like – spring, summer, autumn or winter?

_____

2 Why?

_____

3 **Complete the dialogues.**

1 A: Hi, Jo! What are you doing ?

B: I'm _____ my book.

A: _____ _____

_____ your homework?

B: No, I'm not!!!

2 A: Is it _____?

B: No, it _____ – but it's cold and windy.

A: _____ the boys

_____ football?

B: No, they're _____. They're

_____ TV.

3 A: _____ the weather like?

B: Well, the sun _____

_____.

A: Good. _____ it hot?

B: No, it _____. It

_____ cold.

31

Planet Weather

4b

 1 **Read the description of Paul and Lianne and then draw them.**

Paul is two. He's short and dark. He's wearing a red jumper, blue jeans and trainers
Lianne is Paul's sister. She's twelve. She's tall and fair.
She's wearing a black t-shirt, red trousers and brown sandals.

Paul	Lianne

2 **Look at Paul and Lianne now! Write sentences.**

<u>Paul is wearing Lianne's shoes.</u>

1 _____

2 _____

3 _____

3 **Whose are they? Follow the lines and complete the sentences.**

1 They're the <u>girl's</u>_____ shoes.

2 _____ the teacher's _____ .

3 It's the _____ football strip.

4 _____ the _____ _____ .

5 They're the _____ _____ .

32

Steady Steady Steady Steady Steady Steady

1 **What's Mandy wearing? Write the words in the spaces and find out what she's buying.**

```
   1 □□□□□□ r
  2 □□□□ t
   3 □□□□
  4 □□□□□
5 b □□□□□
```

Mandy is buying _____ .

2 **What are the people wearing?**

Mr Stone   Ted   Carly

1   Mr Stone is wearing _____ .

2   Ted _____ .

3   Carly _____ .

3 **Write *It is* or *They are* and then <u>underline</u> the correct phrases.**

<u>They are</u> the girl's shoes / <u>the girls' shoes</u>.

1   _____ the boy's football / the boys' football.

2   _____ the girl's t-shirt / the girls' T-shirt.

3   _____ the teacher's jacket / the teachers' jacket.

4   _____ the boy's trainers / the boys' trainers.

1 Roberto is 17. He's a student. He's got a sister, Nicola. She's eleven.
Match the words to the pictures and write sentences.

tracksuit   blouse   swimming trunks   shoes   ~~top~~   swimming costume   backpack
leggings   shorts

1   It's Nicola's top.

2   _____

3   _____

4   _____

5   _____

6   _____

7   _____

8   _____

9   _____

2 Write sentences. Look at the example first.

the boys / football

The boys have got a football.

It's the boys' football.

1   the teacher / books

The teacher _____

They're _____

2   the girl / red shoes

_____

_____

3   the boy / blue jeans

_____

_____

4   the girls / clothes

_____

_____

5   the teacher / green jumper

_____

_____

3 Answer the questions.

1   What do you wear on schooldays?

_____

2   What do you wear at weekends?

_____

3   What are you wearing now?

_____

Hot and Cold!

Early Spring
Daffodils shiver,
huddle away from the wind,
like people waiting at a bus stop.

  Adrian Henri

In the sun and shadow
The hands of the sun
are warm on me
when I walk in the open meadow,
But the hands feel cool
when I pass a tree
and walk through the leafy shadow.

  Aileen Fisher

Snow
Feathery soft and quiet the snow,
It covers the road
        and the walk
        and the rooftops
        and whispers to the world:
        Shhhhh!

  Margaret R. Moore.

Questions
1 Which poem do you prefer?
2 What is your favourite season?
3 Write a poem about your favourite season.

Look at the example opposite to help you.

See the new lambs
Passing in the fields
Running
I see the new flowers
Now they are here
Gardens are green

Planet Action

5a

1 Choose the correct words to complete the questions and answers.

| does | do | doesn't | don't | like |
| yes | no | | | |

Does John ♥ like Maths? ☑ Yes , he does.

1 _____ you ♥ _____ tennis?
   ☒ _____ , I _____ .

2 _____ Stella ♥ _____ breakfast?
   ☒ _____ , she _____ .

3 _____ you ♥ _____ football?
   ☑ _____ , I _____ .

4 _____ they ♥ _____ pop music?
   ☑ _____ , they _____ .

5 _____ he ♥ _____ History?
   ☒ _____ , he _____ .

2a Now you! Write six true sentences. Use the words in the box.

can	can't	speak English	sing
use a computer	draw	ski	
dance	play tennis		

I can speak English.

1 I _____

2 I _____

3 I _____

4 I _____

5 I _____

6 I _____

2b Look at the pictures and <u>underline</u> the correct answers.

1 Can he swim?
  Yes, he can. / No, he can't.
  Can she swim?
  Yes, she can. / No, she can't.

2 Can she sing?
  Yes, she can. / No, she can't.
  Do they like it?
  Yes, they do. / No, they don't.

3 Can the girls speak Italian?
  Yes, they can. / No, they can't.
  Can the boy speak Italian?
  Yes, he can. / No, he can't.

4 Can he cook?
  Yes, he can. / No, he can't.
  Does she like it?
  Yes, she does. / No, she doesn't.

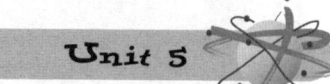

Steady Steady Steady Steady Steady Steady

1a **Look at the table and write sentences.**

| | | ♥ | = like | ✗ | = do not like |
| | | ♥ | = love | ✗✗ | = hate |

	tennis	football	Maths	English	Spanish	computer games
Mandy	♥	✗	♥	♥	♥	✗
Stuart	✗	♥	♥	✗	♥	♥
Craig	♥	♥	✗	♥	♥	♥
Sara	♥	✗	✗	♥	♥	✗
Mr Stone	♥	♥	♥	♥	♥	♥

Mandy / tennis / computer games _Mandy likes tennis but she doesn't like computer games._

1 Stuart / Maths / English _____

2 Craig / English / Spanish _____

3 Mandy and Craig / English / Spanish _____

4 Stuart and Mr Stone / Maths / computer games _____

5 Sara / tennis / computer games _____

1b **Look at the table again and complete the dialogue.**

TEACHER: <u>Do</u> you like English, Mandy?

MANDY: <u>Yes, I do.</u>

TEACHER: And _____ Sara like English?

MANDY: Yes, she _____ English!

TEACHER: Do you like Maths?

MANDY: _____ _____ _____.

TEACHER: _____ Stuart and Craig like Maths?

MANDY: Stuart _____ _____ but Craig _____ _____ _____.

TEACHER: _____ Mr Stone like computer games?

MANDY: He _____ computer games!

2 **Read the passage and answer the questions. Write short answers.**

Ray loves computer games and he loves Maths and football, too. The football teacher likes him. Pam loves Spanish and German. She loves table tennis but she hates football.

Can Ray use a computer? <u>Yes, he can.</u>

1 Does Ray like Maths?

_____

2 Can Ray play football?

_____

3 Can Pam speak foreign languages?

_____

4 Can Pam play table tennis?

_____

5 Does Pam like football?

_____

Go Go Go Go Go Go Go Go Go Go Go Go Go

1 Look at Jenny's bedroom. Read the sentences and correct the mistakes.

Jenny doesn't like jeans.

Yes, she does. She likes jeans.

1 Jenny can't play a musical instrument.

_____

2 Jenny hates chocolate.

_____

3 Jenny doesn't like books.

_____

4 Jenny likes dresses.

_____

5 Jenny can't use a computer.

_____

6 Jenny hates pop music.

_____

2 Complete the questions and answers.

you / breakfast ? (no / like / lunch)

Do you like breakfast?

No, I don't, but I like lunch.

she / English ? (yes / like / Maths)

Does she like English?

Yes, she does, and she likes Maths.

1 they / football ? (no / like / tennis)

_____

_____

2 you / pop music ? (yes / like / jazz)

_____

_____

3 he / computer games ? (no / love / TV)

_____

_____

3a Write about your friend.

_____

_____

_____

_____

3b Write about yourself.

I_____

_____

_____

Planet Action

5b

1 **Make six sentences!**

You He They You I
was wasn't
there were weren't
at
I

I was at home.

1 _____
2 _____
3 _____
4 _____
5 _____
6 _____

2 **Answer the questions. Write sentences.**

1 What day was it yesterday?

It was _____.

_____

2 What was the weather like yesterday?

_____

_____

3 Where were your friends yesterday morning?

_____

_____

4 Where were you at 11 p.m. yesterday?

_____

_____

3 **Read the passage and answer the questions.   True (T) or False (F)?**

It's cold and rainy. George is at home. He's in his room. His friends Kate and Tom are there, too. There's a lot of food in George's room – there are crisps and biscuits and there's some chocolate, too. There's some lemonade and some cola. There's also a lot of pop music! George's mother isn't very happy!

1   It is cold and rainy. | T |
2   George is at school. | |
3   His friends are Anna and Sam. | |
4   There are some crisps. | |
5   There isn't any chocolate. | |
6   George's mother is happy. | |

4 **Now rewrite the passage. Change the verbs into the past.**

It was cold and rainy yesterday.   .

_____

_____

_____

_____

_____

_____

_____

_____

_____

_____

39

Steady Steady Steady Steady Steady Steady

1 Complete the sentences.

Were you at home last Saturday?

No, I <u>wasn't</u>. I <u>was</u> at the shops.

1 _____ _____ sunny?

No, _____ _____ . It was cold and cloudy.

2 _____ _____ any rain?

No, _____ _____ .

3 _____ _____ lots of people there?

Yes, _____ _____ .

4 _____ John there?

No, _____ _____ .

2 Complete the dialogues. Look at the example first.

A: I was terrified.

B: Why <u>were you terrified?</u>

A: Because there <u>wasn't</u> any light.

1 A: She was happy.

B: Why _____ ?

A: Because her friends _____ at the fair.

2 A: They were unhappy.

B: Why _____ ?

A: Because there _____ any food.

3 A: There was panic.

B: Why _____ ?

A: Because there _____ a power cut.

3 Read the passage and write *was* or *were* in the gaps.

Last Saturday there [1] _____ a fair in my town. My friend Karen and I [2] _____ there, but Chris and Ben [3] _____n't. There [4] _____ lots of people there and they [5] _____ very happy. There [6] _____n't a ghost train, but there [7] _____ a big wheel. At night, there [8] _____ lots of lights. It [9] _____ great!

4 Yesterday we were at the supermarket. Look at the picture and answer the questions.

Where was Lianne?

<u>She was next to the entrance.</u>

1 Where was Clive?

_____

2 Where was my dad?

_____

3 Where were my mum and her friend?

_____

4 Where was I???

_____

Go Go Go Go Go Go Go Go Go Go Go Go Go

1 **Read about Bethan's holiday and answer the questions.**

Bethan was on holiday last week. She was in the Lake District, in England. There were a lot of people there. It was very beautiful but the weather wasn't very good. It was cold and rainy and Bethan and her friends were in a tent. There are some very good hotels in the Lake District but Bethan hasn't got a lot of money! Bethan and her friends weren't happy.

1 Where was Bethan last week?

_____

2 Why was she there?

_____

3 What was the weather like?

_____

4 Were the friends in a hotel?

_____

5 Do you like tents?

_____

2 **Where were you last Sunday? What was the weather like? Write sentences.**

1 At 9.00 I was _____

_____ .

The weather was _____

_____ .

2 At 12.00 _____

_____ .

_____ .

3 At 3.00 _____

_____ .

_____ .

4 At 7.00 _____

_____ .

_____ .

5 What time were you in bed?

_____ .

3 **Last week Jo was on holiday in Florida. Look at the pictures and write about Jo's holiday.**

_____

_____

_____

_____

_____

_____

_____

41

William Shakespeare was an English writer who lived around 400 years ago. He lived in Stratford-upon-Avon, a quiet market town, and then he lived in London. Stratford is a very popular place with tourists. They visit Shakespeare's house, and see his plays at the famous theatre. In Shakespeare's time there was no theatre in Stratford, but people watched Shakespeare's plays at the Globe theatre in London. Soldiers destroyed the Globe theatre in 1644, but over 300 years later an American called Sam Wanamaker started to build a new one in the same place. It is finished now and you can see Shakespeare's plays there every summer. In the winter the theatre is closed – because there isn't a roof!!

One of the interesting things about Shakespeare's plays is that when they were performed long ago many of the women had to dress up as men because it was very difficult for women to be actresses. One of his most famous plays is *Romeo and Juliet*. It's a tragic love story and lots of people know the story. Leonardo DiCaprio acted Romeo in a film of the story in 1997. Recently the film *Shakespeare in Love* was a big success all over the world. It tells the story of Shakespeare's life and his plays.

Questions
1 Do you know other plays by Shakespeare?
2 Write about a famous writer from your country.

Planet Action

6a

1 Where can you find these things?
Complete the table.

trains   animals   pictures

food   music   buses

bus station	buses
restaurant	
art gallery	
zoo	
cathedral	
railway station	

2 Read Patrick's letter again on page 42 of your Student's Book. Think about your town or city. Complete the table.

	London	My town/city
an aiport	Heathrow	
a market		
a park		
a museum		
a famous building		

3 Last week, Robbie visited London with his school. Write about their day. Use the verbs in the box.

arrived   learned   loved   travelled
visited   walked

They <u>walked</u> to the station.

1   They _____ by train.

2   They _____ at Paddington Station.

3   They _____ by bus and _____ the London Aquarium.

4   They _____ about sharks.

5   They _____ home again by train.

6   They _____ the day!

Steady Steady Steady Steady Steady Steady

1 Look again at Exercises 2 and 3 in your Student's Book. Find the answers to these clues in the word search below. Write the answers in the gaps.

Heathrow is an <u>airport.</u>

1 Regent's _____ is famous.

2 There's a Picasso at the _____.

3 I liked Camden _____ .

4 We travelled by train from the _____ station.

5 There are lots of animals at the _____ .

6 St Paul's _____ was great!

7 In London the _____ are red.

8 We visited the Natural History _____.

9 We finished the day at a _____ for dinner.

```
p  c  a  t  h  e  d  r  a  l  c
a  i  r  p  o  r  t  a  n  t  s
r  u  m  u  s  e  u  m  o  y  z
k  e  t  b  u  s  e  s  d  c  o
t  m  y  a  w  t  l  m  f  s  o
g  a  r  t  g  a  l  l  e  r  y
t  r  r  y  w  u  z  e  o  s  s
t  k  y  i  a  r  l  c  z  a  w
s  e  k  m  r  a  i  l  w  a  y
n  t  r  a  o  n  o  c  h  e  d
w  k  e  t  l  t  z  l  d  s  r
```

2 Jane travelled from London to Paris by train. Read the sentences about her trip and put them in the correct order.

a ☐ I loved the trip, it was great!

b ☐ After that we travelled by bus to Paris and stayed in a hotel.

c [1] First, we travelled to Waterloo Station by tube.

d ☐ In Paris, we visited the Eiffel Tower and Notre Dame.

e ☐ Finally we travelled home to London by train.

f ☐ Then we travelled to Paris by Eurostar train!

g ☐ We finished our trip at Disneyland, Paris!

3a Write the rule.

To make the past tense of regular verbs, add the letters _____.

3b Write sentences in the past. Use the words below.

person	verb	place	time
I	arrive	restaurant	yesterday
she	finish	a bus station	last week
they	walk	zoo	last weekend
he	travel	airport	last month
we	visit	museum	a few years ago
my brother	stay	London	a month ago

<u>I arrived in London last week.</u>

1 _____

2 _____

3 _____

4 _____

5 _____

Go Go Go Go Go Go Go Go Go Go Go Go Go

1 **Paul travelled to Toronto and Niagara Falls last summer. Look at his itinerary and his comments.**

Day 1	train to London Gatwick plane to Toronto Hotel Bellevue – great!
Day 2	bus to Niagara Falls – fantastic! visit to the CN Tower – amazing! walk along Lake Ontario waterfront
Day 3	visit the Royal Ontario Museum – interesting walk round Eaton Centre – lots of shops home ☹

Complete Paul's letter to his friend.

Dear Jane
How are you? My trip to Toronto was great! First we _____

_____

_____

_____

_____

See you soon, Paul

2 **Write about your trip or holiday. Use the verbs in the box in the past tense.**

arrive   be   finish   hate   learn   like   love   stay   travel   visit   walk

_____

_____

_____

_____

_____

Ready   Ready   Ready   Ready   Ready   Ready

1 **Write short answers.**

Did they go? ✓ Yes, they did.

1 Did you watch TV? ✓

_____

2 Did he travel by car? ✗

_____

3 Was it cold? ✓

_____

4 Were you happy? ✗

_____

5 Were we late? ✗

_____

2 **Rosie is asking Ben about his holiday. Complete the dialogue.**

by	did	didn't	stay	visit
was	you			

ROSIE: Did_____ you visit London?

BEN: Yes, we _____.

ROSIE: _____ _____
_____ Madame Tussaud's?

BEN: No, we _____.

ROSIE: Did _____ walk round
London?

BEN: No, we travelled _____ bus –
it _____ great!

ROSIE: _____ you _____ in
a hotel?

BEN: Yes, we _____. It was great!

3 **Read the passage. Match the questions with the correct answers.**

Last Saturday Ben and his family visited London. They travelled by train to Paddington Station and then walked to a restaurant for lunch. After that they travelled by bus to Big Ben and walked by the River Thames. They stayed in a hotel. In the morning, they travelled by taxi to the Science Museum. Ben loved it. Finally, they travelled by tube to the station because it was time to go home.

1 Where did they travel? e

2 When did they travel there? ☐

3 Did they travel by taxi to the
restaurant? ☐

4 Did they travel by bus? ☐

5 Where did they stay? ☐

6 Where did they travel by taxi? ☐

7 Did Ben like the Science Museum? ☐

8 How did they travel to the station? ☐

a By tube.

b In a hotel.

c Last Saturday.

d No, they walked there.

e They travelled to London.

f To the Science Museum.

g Yes, he loved it!

h Yes, they did. They travelled by bus
to Big Ben.

Steady Steady Steady Steady Steady Steady

1 **Rearrange the words and write the sentences.**

me / grandmother / My / visited / yesterday / .
My grandmother visited me yesterday.

1 didn't / dinner / like / my / today / . / I

   _____

2 loved / John / his / Brazil / holiday / in /.

   _____

3 you / ? / like / Did / London

   _____

4 walk / They / . / didn't / to / school

   _____

5 holiday / Our / was / . / great

   _____

6 cold / was / and / It / rainy / week / . / last

   _____

7 summer / Last / it / hot / . / was

   _____

8 the / walked / . / to / shops / We

   _____

2 **Answer the questions. Write short answers. Be careful!**

Did you go to school last week? _Yes, I did._

1 Did you go on holiday last summer?

   _____

2 Do you like pop music?

   _____

3 Did you watch TV last night?

   _____

4 Did you do your homework last week?

   _____

5 Do you cook at home?

   _____

3a **Claude was in England last month. Write questions to ask her.**

1 how / travel there?
   How did you travel there?

2 where / stay ?

   _____

3 visit / Buckingham Palace?

   _____

4 walk / by the River Thames?

   _____

5 it / cold?

   _____

6 like / London?

   _____

3b **Complete her answers with words from the box. Then match them with the correct questions in Exercise 3a.**

but	by	did	did	didn't	stayed
travelled	was	wasn't	were		

1 ☐ No, it _____. It
   _____ sunny!

2 ☐ Yes, we _____. There
   _____ a lot of people, but
   the Queen wasn't there!

3 ☐1 We _travelled_ there _by_ car.

4 ☐ We _____ in a hotel.

5 ☐ Yes, I _____, _____,
   I didn't like the food.

6 ☐ No, we _____ walk. We
   _____ round London
   _____ bus.

47

1 Read Harry's postcard from London. Harry is home now. Ask him some questions!

We travelled here by ⬛⬛⬛ . The weather is
⬛⬛ and I ⬛⬛⬛ the food. We're staying in
⬛⬛ and it's ⬛⬛⬛ . We visited ⬛⬛⬛
yesterday — it was ⬛⬛⬛ .

See you soon.

Love, Harry

<u>Harry. I can't read your postcard!</u>

<u>How did you travel there?</u>

1 _____ ?

2 _____ ?

3 _____ ?

4 _____ ?

5 _____ ?

6 _____ ?

---

 2 <u>Underline</u> and correct the mistakes in these sentences.

Did Joey <u>travelled</u> by car?   travel

1 I didn't visited the Planetarium.

_____

2 We go to school by foot.

_____

3 I don't stay in a hotel last year.

_____

4 They don't have breakfast yesterday.

_____

5 The weather is terrible yesterday.

_____

6 Was you OK last night?

_____

7 We travelled in car.

_____

8 Did you visited Madrid?

_____

9 We visit Buckingham Palace yesterday.

_____

10 Were the weather cold?

_____

3a Look at the pictures. Complete the questions and answers about Kate's morning.

TRAINS

1 Did you miss the train?
Yes, _____ .

2 Did you wait at the station?
No, I _____ .

3 What _____ ?
Ten thirty!!

4 Why _____ wet?
Because the cars splashed me!

5 Was the teacher angry?
Yes, _____ !

3b Write the story of Kate's terrible morning.

_____

_____

_____

_____

_____

Reading   Reading   Reading   Reading   Reading

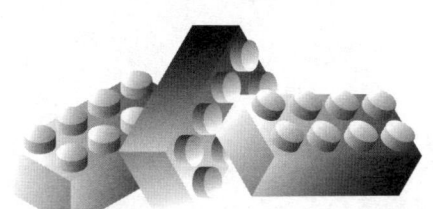

Legoland
Windsor

Legoland is a theme park. The first Legoland is in Denmark, but there is a second Legoland in Windsor, near London in England.

One part of Legoland is called Miniland. It's a model of Europe, made out of toy bricks!! Most of the models are on 1:20 scale. Every day, thousands of visitors from all over the world stand and stare – there are about 800 model buildings and thousands of other moving models; trains, cars, ships, cranes, bridges, fountains and people.

In London, there's Big Ben, the famous clock tower – it's made with 65,000 bricks! The clock sounds the time every hour, all day, every day.

There's Tower Bridge, too, made with 70,000 bricks. It opens for the tall ships on the river!

There are the London underground trains – they move in and out of the station and passengers travel up and down the escalators! Tiny people travel on red London buses and walk in the busy London streets.

Trafalgar Square, St Paul's Cathedral and Buckingham Palace are there too – and lots and lots of other wonderful sights.

London is just a small part of Miniland. You need hours and hours to see all of Europe – the result of 95,000 hours of model making!!! And how many bricks are there in Miniland?
The answer is … 20 million!!

Questions
1   Do you like theme parks?
2   Write about a theme park in your country.

Planet Adventure

7a

1 **Look at the pictures and <u>underline</u> the correct words in each sentence.**

The apple is *on / in* the plate.

1
Mary is *next to / in front of* her bicycle.

2
The shoes are *under / over* the table.

3
My lunch is *on / in* my bag.

4
The girl is in *front of / opposite* the boy.

5
The school is *next to / opposite* the station.

2a **In your town, is there a:**

(tick (✓) the boxes)

☐ post office?   ☐ museum?
☐ railway station?   ☐ supermarket?
☐ shopping centre?   ☐ zoo?
☐ park?   ☐ river?

2b **Look at this map. Write four sentences about the map.**

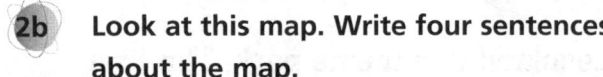
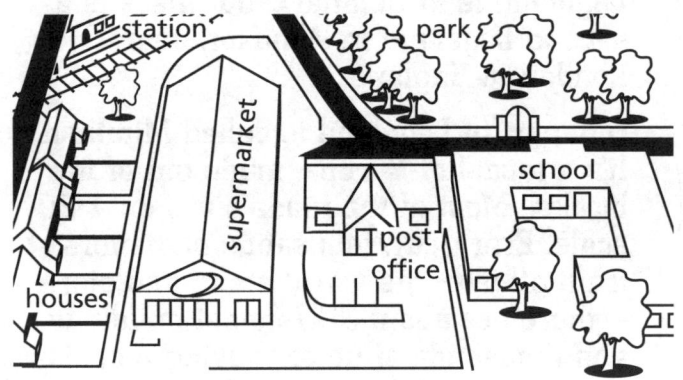

The post office is next to the school.

1 _____
2 _____
3 _____
4 _____

3 **Match the signs to the rules.**

1 BE CAREFUL!
2 STOP!
3 DON'T ENTER!
4 DON'T SMOKE!
5 GO!
6 DON'T DROP LITTER!

Steady Steady Steady Steady Steady Steady

 1 **Read this description and draw the picture!**

There's a river in a park, and there's a bridge over the river. There's a boy under the bridge – in the river! He's swimming because it's very hot. There's a man on the right. He's eating an ice-cream. A girl is on the bridge and she's got a bicycle next to her.

2a **Can you understand the code?**

Danny	Adam	Lianne
Oliver	Charlotte	Carly

Oliver is ✿ Danny and ☆ Charlotte. Charlotte is ✿ Adam and Carly is ✿ Liannne. Carly is ☆ Charlotte and Lianne is ☆ Adam.

✿ = in front of
☆ = next to

2b **Read the passage.**

In our class, John sits ✚ Mary and he also sits ✚ Sam. Mary is on his left and Sam is on his right. Sam is ✿ Oliver. Oliver is behind Sam and ✚ Tom. Tom is on his left. Tom is behind John. John is ✿ Tom. Tom is also ✚ Paul. Paul is behind Mary. Mary is ✚ John and ✿ Paul.

✚ = _____
✿ = _____

2c **Write the names of the pupils in the correct places!**

3 **Choose the correct word to fill each gap.**

clean	do	don't	don't	eat	go
put	speak	talk	wake	wear	

Don't _talk_____ in the lesson!

1 _____ your hand up!
2 _____ English!
3 _____ run!
Who is speaking? _____

4 _Clean_____ your room!
5 _____ to bed!
6 _____ your homework!
7 _____ stay out late!
8 _____ up – it's time for school!
9 _____ a coat!
10 _____ your vegetables!
Who is speaking? _____

1   **Look at the picture and describe it.**

_____   _____

_____   _____

_____   _____

2a   **Read Karl's description of his bedroom.**

> **Useful words**
> alarm clock   baby   box   CD player
> comics   cupboard   floor   toy

In my room there's a bed (of course!), and there are two chairs, a desk and a TV next to the desk. On the desk there are a lot of books and comics. I've got a lot of pens and pencils, too – they're on the desk and on the floor under the bed! My clothes are in the cupboard – and on the chairs and on the floor! I've got a CD player next to my bed, and an alarm clock, too. There are also a lot of toy animals in a box next to my bed, because I liked them when I was a baby – and I still like them now!

Now draw Karl's room.

2b   **Describe your room.**

_____

_____

_____

_____

_____

_____

_____

_____

3   **Read Kenny's instructions how to get from his school to his house. Look at the map and mark his house with a cross (*X*).**

Go out of the school and turn left. There's a bus stop on your left. Wait for the number 9 bus. Get off the bus at the park. My house is opposite the Post Office.

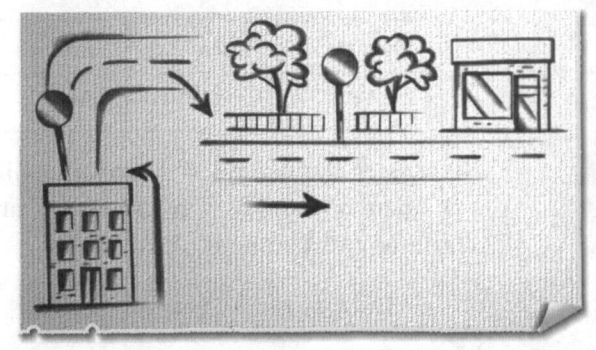

Planet Adventure

7b

Ready Ready Ready Ready Ready Ready

1 True (T) or False (F)?

We mustn't play football in the classroom. ☐T

1 We mustn't talk in class. ☐

2 We must do homework every day. ☐

3 We mustn't eat in class. ☐

4 We mustn't come to school by bicycle. ☐

5 We must come to school at 7.00 a.m. ☐

6 We must clean the classroom every day. ☐

7 We must speak English in English lessons. ☐

2a Match the signs to the rules.

a ☒ b ✋ c ☒

1 Drive on the right.
2 You mustn't eat here.
3 You must wash your hands.

2b Draw signs for these rules.

1 You must speak English.
2 You mustn't wear shoes.
3 You must wear a helmet.

☐ ☐ ☐

2c Write the sentences from Exercise 2a and 2b as 'dos' and 'donts'.

Don't eat here!

1 _____

2 _____

3 _____

4 _____

5 _____

3 What are the rules at a swimming pool? Write four rules. Use the words in the box and the pictures to help you.

run   wash your feet   wear shoes
wear a costume or trunks!

1 You mustn't _____

2 You _____

3 You _____

4 You _____

53

Steady   Steady   Steady   Steady   Steady   Steady

 1a **Look at the poster. What does it mean? Tick (✓) the best idea.**

Don't travel by train! ☐

Don't play on the railway! ☐

You must travel by train. ☐

You must play football. ☐

1b **Write two rules for each of these places.**

A kitchen

1 *You must not touch matches.*

2 _____

  _____

A railway station

1 _____

  _____

2 _____

  _____

A hospital

1 _____

  _____

2 _____

  _____

2 **Unjumble the words to make rules.**

1 oukustywmal

  You must walk.

2 ouusspgyeakEnlismht

  _____

3 omiusn'tdiyvetguonrherht

  _____

4 ougemyusottoedarlby

  _____

5 ylon'tumusttak

  _____

Now match the rules with the following instructions.

a Don't run.

  You must walk.

b Don't go to bed late.

  _____

c Be quiet.

  _____

d Don't speak Spanish.

  _____

e Drive on the left.

  _____

Go Go Go Go Go Go Go Go Go Go Go Go Go

1 **Look at the pictures and write rules.**

Useful words
boiling water   cooker   knife   matches

1 The children must not play with the matches.
_____
_____
_____
_____

2 _____
_____
_____
_____

 2 **Complete the rules for the zoo. Look at the picture on page 50 of your Student's Book.**

You _mustn't_____ play with the dolphins.

1 You _____ touch the
_____ .

2 You _____ wake the
_____ up.

3 You _____ carry a
_____ .

4 You _____ keep the zoo
_____ .

5 You _____ _____ the
monkeys.

6 You _____ follow the
_____ .

 3 **Write six rules for your perfect school.**

You mustn't do any homework._____
You must wear jeans._____

1 _____
2 _____
3 _____
4 _____
5 _____
6 _____

Reading   Reading   Reading   Reading   Reading

Marylebone Station is a very busy stop on the London Underground. There you can visit two very famous tourist attractions.

Madame Tussaud's is very, very popular – but be careful! There are always very long queues, you must get there early and be patient! It's an amazing place, full of famous people – all models, of course!

Madame Tussaud lived in Paris and also in Britain about 200 years ago. She made wax models of famous people. Her models were very popular – remember, there was no television or cinema then.

The building we call 'Madame Tussaud's' is a museum and it opened in 1884. There was a terrible fire there in 1925 and a lot of models melted! The building didn't close, though, and it is now a 'must' for every visitor to London. There you can see politicians, kings and queens, actors, pop stars, scientists ... the list is endless. There are lots of guides at Madame Tussaud's – but watch out! Not all of them are real!

The London Planetarium is next to Madame Tussaud's and most tourists visit both places. It's an enormous dome, and inside you can see star shows and learn about the universe. There are also models of planets, satellites and spacecraft. It's a great place for people of all ages!

Questions

1 Have you visited a museum like this? Where? Did you like it?
2 Write about a popular museum in your country.

Planet Adventure

8a

 Look at the pictures and write sentences.

(have a meal)

They're going to have a meal.

(correct the books)

1 _____

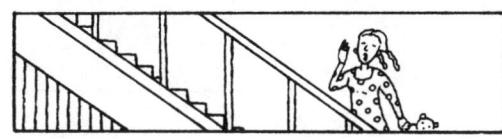

(go to bed)

2 _____

(watch a film)

3 _____

(drink some water)

4 _____

(go on holiday)

5 _____

 Write questions with *going to*.

he / to school?

Is he going (to go) to school?

1 you / go on holiday?

_____

2 you / buy a new bike?

_____

3 she / dance?

_____

4 they / score a goal?

_____

5 he / do his homework?

_____

3 **Answer the questions. Write *Yes, I am.* or *No, I'm not.***

1 Are you going to school tomorrow?

_____

2 Are you going to do any homework tomorrow?

_____

3 Are you going to watch TV tonight?

_____

4 Are you going on holiday next year?

_____

5 Are you going to leave school this year?

_____

1 Write questions.

John's going to visit a friend.

(Julie) <u>Is he going to visit Julie?</u>

1 I'm going to have a drink.

(cola) _____?

2 Mr Stone is going to teach tomorrow.

(Maths) _____

_____?

3 My parents are going to buy a present.

(a new CD) _____

_____?

4 My sister is going on holiday tomorrow.

(Ireland) _____

_____?

5 We're going to see a film.

(Star Wars) _____

_____?

2 Complete the dialogues.

1 A: Hi! <u>Are</u> _____ you

<u>going to go</u> _____ (go)

to Peter's party tomorrow?

B: Yes, _____ _____.

A: _____ (take)

a present?

B: _____

some flowers for his mother.

A: Good idea!

2 A: _____ Kate and Jonathan

_____ (buy)

a new computer tomorrow?

B: No, _____.

A: What _____?

B: _____ a new TV.

3 A: _____ Mr Stone

_____ (be)

our teacher next year?

B: No, _____. We

_____ (have)

a new teacher.

3 Write true sentences about your plans for next week. Use the ideas in the box to help you.

buy a new CD	buy new clothes
clean my bedroom	cook the dinner
go to the cinema	write a letter
walk to school	
speak English every day	
stay away from school	
telephone a friend	
visit my grandmother	

<u>I'm not going to buy a new CD.</u>

_____

_____

_____

_____

Go Go Go Go Go Go Go Go Go Go Go Go Go

1 **Write questions for the answers.**

<u>Are you going to go to the cinema tonight?</u>
No, we're not going to the cinema – we're going to watch TV.

1 _____
_____?
No, he's going to be home early.

2 _____
_____?
They're going to France for their next holidays.

3 _____
_____?
I'm going to travel round the world and then I'm going to university.

4 _____
_____?
I'm going to be a doctor.

5 _____
_____?
It's going to rain all day tomorrow.

2 **Read the situations and answer the questions, using your own ideas. Write sentences.**

Harry is walking into a supermarket. He's very hungry. What's he going to do?

<u>He's going to buy some food.</u>

1 Mandy and Sue are wearing new clothes. They've got some tickets. Where are they going to go?

_____
_____

2 A mother is putting a baby into a car. The baby is crying. Where are they going to go?

_____
_____

3 A man is wearing a football shirt and scarf. He's walking into a stadium. What's he going to do?

_____
_____

4 A boy is buying some flowers. His girl friend is outside the shop. What's he going to do?

_____
_____

5 A woman is buying some flour, eggs and milk. What's she going to make?

_____
_____

3 **It's January 1st. Oliver is writing his New Year's Resolutions.**

<u>I'm going to help my mother.</u>
<u>I'm not going to be late for school.</u>

Write four resolutions for yourself!!

1 _____
2 _____
3 _____
4 _____

Planet Adventure

8b

1 **Complete the dialogues.**

(Star Wars)   <u>Let's go and see Star Wars!</u>

 <u>That's a good idea!</u>

1 (play chess) _____

   (watch TV) _____

   _____

2 (drink water) _____

   (cola) _____

   _____

(pizza)   <u>Shall we eat pizza?</u>

(burgers)   <u>Oh no! Let's have burgers.</u>

3 (play on the computer)

   _____

   _____

4 (do our homework) _____

   (play football) _____

   _____

2 **Karl and Jon are planning a trip. What are they saying? Use the verbs in the box.**

> eat   go by   go on   ~~go to~~   stay
> take   visit

a leisure park! (Let's)

<u>Let's go to a leisure park!</u>

1 sandwiches (Why don't we)

   _____

2 the big wheel (Shall we)

   _____

3 lots of ice cream (Let's)

   _____

4 the zoo (Shall we)

   _____

5 bus (Why don't we)

   _____

6 all day (Let's)

   _____

3 **Find the adjectives to match the nouns below in the wordsearch. Write the adjectives in the correct place.**

c	i	r	a	n	s	a	r	c	p
l	r	t	f	o	h	e	i	p	l
d	c	i	g	a	r	t	o	u	m
u	o	e	r	i	n	o	a	e	d
s	d	r	l	a	l	o	s	d	e
d	r	a	m	a	t	i	c	e	r
r	c	o	m	i	c	m	t	s	t
d	r	m	r	d	o	i	o	c	y
o	r	o	e	s	r	l	s	k	a
i	s	r	l	d	i	r	p	u	r
g	k	o	r	d	s	a	i	s	m

comedy   <u>comic</u> _____

drama   _____

music   _____

romance _____

tragedy _____

60

Steady Steady Steady Steady Steady Steady

1 **What do you think? Read the following suggestions, and write your responses!**

Let's have a holiday! <u>That's a good idea.</u>

1 Shall we do lots of homework tonight?

   _____

2 Why don't we have a pizza tonight?

   _____

3 Let's go to the shops tomorrow.

   _____

4 Why don't we clean our bedrooms?

   _____

5 Shall we buy some ice cream?

   _____

6 Let's have a party!

   _____

7 Why don't we play football?

   _____

8 Shall we speak English all day tomorrow?

   _____

2 **Read the TV guide and complete the dialogue.**

> **6.30 – 7.00   Channel 1**
> **What a Laugh!**
> Comedy show for kids.
>
> **6.45 – 9.00   Channel 2**
> **International Football**
> Manchester United v Deportivo
>
> **6.50 – 7.15   Channel 3**
> **Secret Life of Cats**
> Cat lovers must watch this!!
>
> **7.00 – 7.30   Channel 1**
> **Clever Cooking**
> Today we learn to make easy cakes.
>
> **7.15 – 7.45   Channel 3**
> **James Bond 007**
> Don't miss this one!
>
> **7.45 – 9.30   Channel 3**
> **Pop 2000**
> All your favourite bands. Enjoy!!!

JOHN: What <u>shall</u> _____ we watch?

KATE: _____ watch the programme about cooking. I love cakes!

PAUL: Oh no! I hate cooking. Why

   _____ _____

   watch the James Bond film?

JOHN: _____ _____!
   Let's watch the football.

PAUL: That's a good _____.

KATE: I'm going out.

3 **Read the following descriptions of films. Choose the correct word to fill each gap.**

> comedy   comic   dramatic   musical
> romance   romantic   tragedy
> tragic

1 The boy and girl are in love, it's very

   _____!

2 There's lots of singing and dancing. It's a

   _____.

3 It was really sad. It's a _____ story.

4 We laughed all evening! A great

   _____.

5 It's a _____ story with lots of action.

6 The film *Titanic* is a _____.

7 It was a _____ film and we all laughed and laughed.

8 I like _____, I loved the film *Notting Hill*.

1 **You and your friends are going to have a party. Make some suggestions.**

1 When shall we have the party?

_____

2 Where shall we have the party?

_____

3 Who shall we invite?

_____

4 What shall we eat?

_____

5 What shall we drink?

_____

6 What music shall we have?

_____

7 What time shall we finish the party?

_____

2 **You are going out with your friend. She's making some suggestions. What do you think?**

Let's go to the library.

Oh no! Why don't we go to the swimming pool.

1 Why don't we buy some new clothes?

_____

2 Shall we stay at home and do our homework?

_____

3 Let's stay at home and cook the dinner!

_____

4 Shall we stay at home and watch TV?

_____

5 Why don't we go for a walk?

_____

3a **Read the reviews and answer the questions.**

_____

Fire is an adventure film. There's a lot of action and the actors are really good, especially Phil Hancock. One problem for me was the music. It was very loud and I didn't like it. The photography was brilliant and the special effects (that car chase!!!) were brilliant. You must see it.

_____

Remember My Land is a sad love story. It's very romantic and I loved the music – but it wasn't a happy ending, and I wasn't happy at all! Go and see it, but don't go alone, and take lots of tissues!

_____

1 True (T) or False (F)?

a The writer enjoyed _Fire_. ☐

b The writer liked the music in _Fire_. ☐

c Fire is an exciting film. ☐

d _Remember my Land_ is funny. ☐

2 Why does it say 'take lots of tissues!'?

_____

3b **Write a review of a film you know.**

_____

_____

_____

_____

_____

_____

Reading   Reading   Reading   Reading   Reading

TV CHOICE

Drama

Casualty

8.05 BBC1

You must have a lot of handkerchiefs for this one! This week's hospital drama revolves around two teenagers and their parents. An accident brings them all to Holby Hospital, and then the drama really starts!!

Nature

The Natural World

5.45 BBC2

This documentary is very dry!! It's about a desert in Namibia, Africa. There, years go by with no rain at all, and it can be 167°F! There are animals here – elephants, giraffes, lizards and others. The film shows these creatures looking for food and water in this difficult land. Amazing photography. Don't miss this wonderful programme.

Walking with Dinosaurs

8.30 BBC1

A breathtaking programme. It shows us giant reptiles in the sea. They swim, eat, fight and play. They aren't real (of course) – but they are very, very life-like!!

Film

My Uncle the Alien

8.30 Channel 5

The US President's young daughter runs away from her bodyguards and explores Los Angeles. She sees poor people and helps them and she meets a new friend, too. This film is very sentimental, but it's good entertainment.

Questions

1   What is your favourite TV programme?
2   Why do you like it?

Planet Holiday

Ready   Ready   Ready   Ready   Ready   Ready

 1 Choose the correct word to complete each text.

> doesn't   have   dreaming   drives   driving   has   is   is   ~~is~~   is   is   is
> isn't   playing   plays   sleeping

Dave [1] <u>is</u> a taxi driver. He [2] _____ people to and from Heathrow airport. He's on holiday today. He [3] _____ [4] _____, he [5] _____ [6] _____ on the beach.

Kelly [1] _____ a musician. She [2] _____ the violin in an orchestra. It's Saturday evening and she [3] _____ [4] _____ some Mozart.

Samantha [1] _____ a supermodel.
She [2] _____ [3] _____ breakfast and for lunch she [4] _____ a carrot and hot water.
She [5] _____ [6] _____ of chocolate cake.

 2 Read the texts in Exercise 1 again and complete the table.

	every day	now
Dave		
Kelly	he drives	
Samantha		
You		

Steady Steady Steady Steady Steady Steady

 1 **Read the sentences and <u>underline</u> the correct words.**

1 My father <u>teaches</u> / is teaching Maths. He's working / <u>He works</u> in the garden at the weekends.

2 I get up / am getting up at 7 in the week and at 9 at weekends.

3 How do you travel / are you travelling to school every morning?

4 It doesn't rain / isn't raining today.

5 Where is he coming / does he come from?

6 What clothes do you wear / are you wearing at weekends?

7 They don't go / aren't going to school, they are 19.

8 Sandy is going / goes to school but she works / is working in a shop on Saturday mornings.

9 Zed Frankly is a rock singer. He isn't singing / doesn't sing now, he's sleeping / sleeps in his hotel room.

10 Anna lives / is living in Toronto but she stays / is staying in New York this week.

 2 **Answer the questions. Write short answers.**

Do you go to school? <u>Yes I do.</u>

1 Do you like English?

_____

2 Are you at school?

_____

3 Do you wear jeans to school?

_____

4 Are you wearing a coat?

_____

 3 **Read the passage and answer the questions.**

Zed Frankly is a singer. He's 19 and he sings in the band 'Zapp!' The band plays in clubs and they also play at concerts. Zed doesn't play a musical instrument but his friend Alph plays the guitar. Zed wears black clothes and Alph wears black, too. They live in New York but at the moment they're on tour in London. They're staying in a big hotel. It's 11.30 a.m. in England and Zed is sleeping. He doesn't get up in the morning!!!

1 Does Zed play the guitar?

<u>No, he doesn't.</u>

2 Do Zed and Alph wear black?

_____

3 Does Alph live in New York?

_____

4 Are Zed and Alph at home at the moment?

_____

5 What is Zed doing?

_____

1 **Maisie is interviewing Zed Frankly. Look at Maisie's questions and the chart and complete the dialogue.**

Free time?   Music?   Clothes?   Where live?

Name	Zed Frankly
Job	Singer
Home	New York
Hobbies	sleeping, music
Favourite music	his own music!
Favourite colour	black
Favourite clothes	black clothes!

MAISIE: 1 _____

_____ ?

ZED: I sleep a lot, and I 2 _____
music.

MAISIE: 3 _____

_____ ?

ZED: My music, of course!

MAISIE: Oh, right. And 4 _____

_____ ?

ZED: 5 _____

New York, but 6 _____

here in London this week.

MAISIE: 7 _____

black clothes all the time, Zed?

ZED: Yes, I 8 _____ .

It's my favourite colour!

2 **Read about Teresa and Robin and answer the questions.**

Teresa and Robin live in Oxford. They are teachers. Robin teaches Music and Teresa teaches English. Every day Robin cycles to work and Teresa travels by car. Robin's brother lives in Wales. He's got a big house and in the holidays Teresa and Robin go and stay with him. They love the countryside there, and they go for lots of walks. It's not holiday time at the moment, but next weekend they're going to go to Wales and they're going to climb Mount Snowdon.

1   Where do Robin and Teresa live?

_____

2   What do they do?

_____

3   Where do they go on holiday?

_____

4   How does Robin travel to work?

_____

5   Where are they at the moment?

_____

6   What are they going to do next weekend?

_____

3 **Now you! Write about yourself and your friends. Write about:**

• clothes (What do you wear to school? What are you wearing now?)
• music (What do you like? Are you listening to music now?)
• food (What do you like? Are you eating or drinking now?)
• TV (What programmes do you watch? Are you watching TV now?)

_____

_____

_____

_____

_____

Planet Holiday

9b

Ready Ready Ready Ready Ready Ready

1 Complete the passage with the verbs in the past simple.

Danny [1] _____ (start) a new school in 1992. He [2] _____ (be) eleven. A lot of the other children [3] _____ (be) new pupils, too. Danny [4] _____ (travel) to school by train and then [5] _____ (walk) from the station to school. He [6] _____ (like) the train journey but he [7] _____ (not like) the walk. His favourite lessons [8] _____ (be) Maths and Music. He [9] _____ (play) the drums in the school orchestra. He [10] _____ (hate) Sport because he [11] _____ (not like) the teacher. Danny [12] _____ (pass) his examinations in 1999 and now he is studying Maths at university.

2 Match the questions to the answers.

1 Did you travel by bus?
2 Did you like school?
3 Did you play in the school orchestra?
4 When did you pass your exams?
5 What were your favourite subjects?

a In 1999.
b Maths and Music.
c Yes, I did – but I didn't like Sport.
d No, I travelled by train.
e Yes, I did. I played the drums.

3 Write about what you did in school last year. Use the words in the boxes to help you.

| pass travel play like |

| bus train car Maths piano football tennis examinations |

_____
_____
_____
_____

67

Steady   Steady   Steady   Steady   Steady   Steady

1a **Look at the information about George's holiday last year. Write sentences.**

Where was your holiday?
Canada
When was it?
last August
How did you travel?
plane
Who travelled with you?
My parents and my sister
Where did you stay?
A hotel in Vancouver
Did you like it?
Yes!!!
Did you like the food?
Yes, it was great!
Are you going again?
No. We're going to stay at home.

George's holiday was in Canada.

_____

_____

_____

_____

_____

_____

_____

1b **Read Sally's answers. Write the questions.**

1 _____?
We were in Paris for our holiday last year.

2 _____?
No, we didn't. I don't like planes. We travelled by car.

3 _____?
We stayed with friends, near the Eiffel Tower.

4 _____?
My mother and my brother.

5 _____?
Yes, we did. We loved all the food.

6 _____?
Yes, we did – it was great.

7 _____?
No, we're not. We're going to Florida next year.

2 **Now write about a holiday you had. Write about these things:**

- place (Where did you go?)
- time (When did you go?)
- travel (How did you travel?)
- people (Who travelled with you?)
- place (Where did you stay?)
- food (What did you eat? Did you enjoy it?)

_____

_____

_____

_____

_____

Go Go Go Go Go Go Go Go Go Go Go Go Go

1 **Look at the holiday advertisements.**

Superthrills
the leisure park of the future!
Do you like frightening rides? Our rides are fantastic!
Our **Monster Water Double Loop** takes you on a wet and wonderful 20 minute ride – it's the only one like this in Europe!
The Turbo Skyrocket shoots you into orbit – and back (upside down).
Come to Superthrills (only for the brave!)

Visit wonderful **SCOTLAND!**
There's a lot to see and learn in Scotland. Come and explore the fantastic castles, enjoy the beautiful countryside, taste our wonderful food, meet the friendly people. The shops are great, too! You're going to love it!

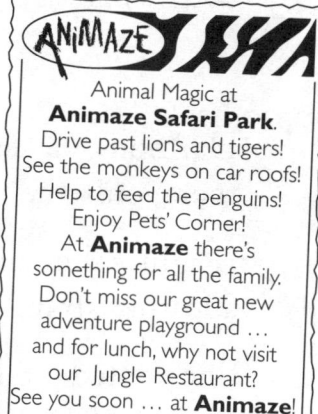

ANIMAZE
Animal Magic at **Animaze Safari Park**. Drive past lions and tigers! See the monkeys on car roofs! Help to feed the penguins! Enjoy Pets' Corner! At **Animaze** there's something for all the family. Don't miss our great new adventure playground … and for lunch, why not visit our Jungle Restaurant? See you soon … at **Animaze**!

Choose a day trip for the following people and say why.

- James and Euan are twelve. They like adventure.
- Carly and Kate are thirteen. Their brother Jo is nine. They love animals.
- Mary and Greg are thirteen. They like History.
- Sam and Frank are eleven. They are looking for excitement.

A good day trip for James and Euan is to
Superthrills, because there are frightening
rides and they like adventure.

1   A good day trip for Carly and Kate is to
_____
_____

2   A good day trip for Mary and Greg is to
_____
_____

3   A good day trip for Sam and Frank is to
_____
_____

2 **Read part of a letter from your friend.**

We travelled all over the country and we visited a lot of places. We stayed in a great place but we didn't like the food. Alice wasn't very happy.

Write to your friend, and ask some questions about the holiday. Use the words in the box.

| how | what | where | why |

_____
_____
_____
_____
_____
_____
_____

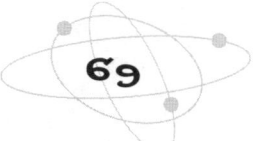

69

Reading Reading Reading Reading Reading

D. K. Smith   *The Queen's Nose*

Harmony picked up the magic coin. She looked around, but no one was there, only the postman at the end of the road.

"Right," she said, "I wish for a large wristwatch, digital, with the date and a leather strap."

She waited a moment and then stared at her left wrist. Nothing happened. She didn't hear the voice from the footpath.

"Good morning," said the postman.

"Oh, sorry. Good morning."

"Do you live here?" asked the postman.

"Yes."

"Name of Parker?"

"Yes."

"You can take your post and save my feet." He handed Harmony some letters and a parcel.

Harmony looked at the post. There were three letters for her father, and a postcard. She turned the parcel over. It was for her.

Harmony opened the parcel and looked. Inside the brown paper was a white box. Inside the white box was a large wristwatch, digital, with the date and a leather strap.

Question
Imagine you can wish for one thing. What is it? Why?

Planet Holiday

10a

1 Write five things you can do and five things you can't do! Use the ideas in the box or your own ideas.

> cook   draw   paint   play the piano
> drive a car   ride a bike   ride a horse
> roller skate   sing   skateboard   ski
> speak English   speak Italian   swim
> use a computer

I can …

_____

_____

_____

_____

_____

I can't …

_____

_____

_____

_____

2a Jake is going to start university next week. Look at his list and write the things he must do and the things he mustn't do!

> eat fruit ✓
> get up early ✓
> go to bed late ✗
> go to night clubs ✗
> go to the library ✓
> sleep all day ✗
> smoke ✗
> study ✓
> wash his clothes ✓
> get up late ✗

1   He must eat fruit. _____

2   _____

3   _____

4   _____

5   _____

6   He mustn't go to bed late. _____

7   _____

8   _____

9   _____

10 _____

2b What must you do next weekend? What mustn't you do? Write four sentences.

1   I must _____

2   I must _____

3   I mustn't _____

4   I mustn't _____

1a What's the matter? Look at the pictures and write sentences. Use the verbs in the box to help you.

find   hear   ride   sleep
understand   speak

1   She can't _____ .

2   He can't _____

3   _____

4   _____

5   _____

6   _____

1b Can you do that? Look at the picture of Nick and write five sentences.

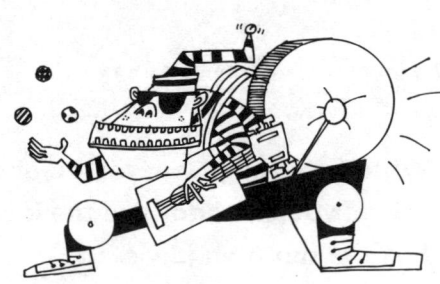

He can juggle but I can't.

He can juggle and I can, too.

1   _____

2   _____

3   _____

4   _____

5   _____

2 How many sentences can you make?

1   Canadian drivers / English drivers   must / mustn't   drive on the   right / left
Canadian drivers must drive on the right.
_____
_____
_____

2   Drivers   must / mustn't   stop / go at a   green / red   light
_____
_____
_____
_____

3   You must / mustn't   speak English / French   in an English / a French conversation class
_____
_____
_____
_____

Go Go Go Go Go Go Go Go Go Go Go Go Go

1 John is looking at the school noticeboard. Look at the questions on the School Orchestra poster. Write some questions for posters 1–4.

BOATS Club
_____
_____
_____
_____
_____
_____

French Conversation Club
_____
_____
_____
Join us!!

RIDING CLUB
_____
_____
_____
You're going to love the riding club!!

Cookery Club
_____
_____
_____
_____
_____
Come and cook

School Orchestra

Do you like classical music?

Can you play an instrument?

Join the orchestra!!

2 Write two rules for each club. Use the ideas in the box to help you.

play a musical instrument
practise at home   speak English
speak French   stand behind the horses
stand up in the boats   wash your hands
wear a life jacket   wear a riding hat
wear an apron

1 School Orchestra
You must play a musical instrument.
_____

2 Boats Club
_____
_____

3 French Conversation Club
_____
_____

4 Riding Club
_____
_____

5 Cooking Club
_____
_____

3a Design a poster for The School Choir.

[blank poster box]

3b Write two rules for The School Choir.

1 _____

2 _____

Ready   Ready   Ready   Ready   Ready   Ready

 1 **Look at the pictures and write responses and suggestions.**

Let's have pizza!

No, I don't like pizza. Let's have burgers!

1   Shall we go to the shops?

_____

2   Why don't we play football?

_____

3   Let's go to the beach!

_____

4   Shall we eat at the restaurant?

_____

2 **What are you/aren't you going to do tomorrow? Write sentences.**

> do my homework   go to school
> play computer games   speak English
> stay in bed   travel by train   watch TV

✓   _I'm going to go to school._

_____

_____

✗   _I'm not going to stay in bed._

_____

_____

3 **Find the code for the days of the week.**

Jlkaxv = Monday

A	B	C	D	E	F	G	H	I	J	K	L	M

N	O	P	Q	R	S	T	U	V	W	X	Y	Z

_____ = Tuesday

_____ = Wednesday

_____ = Thursday

_____ = Friday

_____ = Saturday

_____ = Sunday

What does this message mean?

Pexii tb dl ql qeb zfkbjx qljloolt?

_____

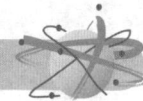

Steady Steady Steady Steady Steady Steady

1 **Look at the poster.**

English Club

We are going to start an
English club. Can you help us?
Have you got any ideas or

suggestions about:

• activities •

• food and drink •

Please help!!!!!

**Wendy and Mikki are talking about the
English Club. Write the dialogue. Write
suggestions and responses.**

WENDY: (read some English books)

Let's read some English books.

MIKKI: ✗ (read some magazines)

Oh no! Why don't we read some

magazines?

WENDY: ✓ _That's a good idea._

WENDY (watch some English films)

_____

MIKKI: ✓ (speak English all the time)

_____

WENDY ✗ (listen to English pop music)

_____

MIKKI: ✓ (have English food)

_____

WENDY ✗ (have Chinese food)

_____

MIKKI: ✓ (drink English tea)

_____

WENDY _Hmmm ..._

2 **Rearrange the words to make questions,
and then write your answers.**

time / you / to / get / What / up / going /
tomorrow / are / morning / ?

What time are you going to get up

tomorrow morning?

I'm going to get up at 7.30.

1 are / going / to / What / tomorrow / do /
   evening / you / ?

_____

_____

2 visit / you / to / a / friend / weekend / ? /
   Are / this / going

_____

_____

3 tonight / you / going / watch / Are / TV/ ?
   / to

_____

_____

4 you / to / going / go / the / shops / Are /
   next / ? / Saturday / to

_____

_____

3 **Bernie is going on holiday to Spain. What is
/ isn't he going to do? Write four sentences.**

eat English food   eat paella
get up early   go to discos
lie on the beach   read lots of books
speak Spanish   swim in the sea
visit lots of museums   watch TV

He's going to lie on the beach. He isn't going to

eat English food.

1 _____

2 _____

3 _____

4 _____

75

Go Go Go Go Go Go Go Go Go Go Go Go Go

1a Read part of a letter from a friend and write your reply.

> It's Freddie's birthday so let's do something special! But what shall we do? Shall we go out, or shall we have a party? What shall we give him? What do you think?

_____

_____

_____

_____

_____

_____

_____

1b Tell your friends about your plans for Freddie's birthday. Use your ideas from 1a.

We're going to _____

_____

_____

_____

_____

2 Look at the poster and complete the dialogue.

ANDY: Are you _____ to buy a ticket?

PETE: I _____ know. _____ you like magic shows?

ANDY: _____, I do. I'm going _____ go on Tuesday.

PETE: I'm _____ to the cinema on Tuesday. Why _____ we go on _____?

ANDY: OK. _____ get the tickets now.

PETE: Ummm. I haven't _____ any money.

ANDY: Oh …

Amazing Buildings

The Great Pyramid is in Egypt. It is about $4\frac{1}{2}$ thousand years old and still a mystery. Inside the pyramid there are secret passages. They go to … an empty room. Was it for a dead king? Where is the body? Nobody knows, but there are lots of strange stories. Some people believe it is full of magic, others say it is very unlucky. What do *you* think?

The Millennium Dome is next to the River Thames, in London. It's very new, very expensive … and very, very big. It's one kilometre all the way round, and 50 metres high. Inside, there's room for the Statue of Liberty or even the Great Pyramid (lying down)!

The Statue of Liberty is famous all over the world. It is 93 metres high and stands in New York harbour. It is over a hundred years old, and although it is made of copper, it is green these days! It was a gift from the French people to the American people. The designer was Gustave Eiffel – he was also the builder of France's famous Eiffel Tower. The statue has got a real woman's face – the face of the sculptor's mother! The statue has also got a door in her right foot, and visitors can climb up a staircase and stand inside her head. From there, they can see a fantastic view.

Another new and modern building is the Guggenheim Museum in Bilbao. It is built with stone, glass and a metal called titanium. One side of the building runs to the Nervión River, 16 metres below the level of the city.

It is more than 50 metres high and is in the centre of the city. You can enter the building from one of the main streets, Calle Iparraguirre. The longest gallery in the museum is 130 metres long!

Questions
1   Do you know any fantastic buildings?
2   Write about a famous building in your country.

Key word list

Unit 1

Colours

blue
brown
green
orange
white
yellow

Objects for school

bag
book
cassette
pen
pencil
pencil-case
rubber
ruler

Personal details

name
address
age
surname
boy
telephone number
girl
short
tall
dark
fair

Personality

friendly/unfriendly
happy/unhappy
romantic/unromantic
generous/mean
kind/unkind
serious/fun

Unit 2

Parts of the day

morning
afternoon
evening
night

Time

it's one/two/three o'clock
it's quarter past four/five/six
it's half past seven/eight/nine
it's quarter to ten/eleven/twelve
it's midday
it's midnight

Daily routine

get up
have breakfast
brush your teeth
go to school
have lunch
watch TV
have dinner
go to bed
cook
play
read
clean

Family

mother
father
brother
sister
son
daughter
grandfather
baby
parent

Unit 3

Animals

antelope
bear
bird
cat
crocodile
dog
elephant
fish
lion
monkey
ostrich
sheep
snake

Food

apple
bread
burger
butter
cake
carrot
cheese
chips
egg
fish
hamburger
meat
milk
oil
orange
peach
pizza
potato
rice
sandwich
tomato

Places to eat

canteen
restaurant

Unit 4

Weather

hot
cold
cloud
cloudy
fog
foggy
rain (n)
rain (v)
rainy
snow (n)
snow (v)
snowy
sun
sunny
wind
windy

Clothes

bag
boots
cardigan
coat
dress
gloves
hat
jacket
jeans
scarf
shirt
shoes
skirt
sweater
T-shirt
trousers
umbrella

People and fashion

gothic
heavy metal
hippy
punk

Unit 5

Verbs expressing preference

like
love
hate

Interests

CD
computer
computer game
cook (v)
dance (v)
disco
English
French
German
golf
jazz
musical instrument
paint (v)
play (v)
rock (n)
sing
ski (v)
Spanish
speak
swim (v)
table tennis
tennis
use (v)

Unit 6

Places in a city

airport
art gallery
bus station
cathedral
market
museum
park
railway station
restaurant
zoo

Verbs for describing a visit or a trip

arrive
finish
learn
love
return
start
stay
travel
visit
walk

Transport

bike
boat
bus
car
coach
plane
taxi
train
tube

Unit 7

Prepositions

behind	next to
in front of	opposite
on (the right)	under
on (the left)	

Places in a town

car park	railway station
park	river
post office	sports centre

Unit 8

Space/technology

Earth	star
galaxy	sun
moon	technology
solar	water
space	wind

Words for describing films

(nouns)	(adjectives)
comedy	comic
drama	dramatic
romance	romantic
tragedy	tragic
adventure	
musical	
science fiction	

Unit 9

Places to stay and visit on holiday

beach	farm
camping site	mountains
country	theme park

Verbs for describing a holiday

climb	visit
organize	walk
stay	

Unit 10

Verbs/phrases for describing holiday activities

canoe	ski
do gymnastics	snowboard
do judo	swim
ride a bike	windsurf
skateboard	

Days of the week

Monday
Tuesday
Wednesday
Thursday
Friday
Saturday
Sunday

Macmillan Education
Between Towns Road, Oxford OX4 3PP
A division of Macmillan Publishers Limited
Companies and representatives throughout the world

ISBN 0 333 95028 3

Text © Liz Kilbey, Sue Mohamed, Sagrario Salaberri,
Carmen Fernández Santás 2001
Design and illustration © Macmillan Publishers Limited 2001

First published 2001

All rights reserved; no part of this publication may be
reproduced, stored in a retrieval system, transmitted in any
form, or by any means, electronic, mechanical, photocopying,
recording, or otherwise, without the prior written permission
of the publishers.

Produced by Moondisks Ltd, Cambridge
Illustrated by: Phillip Burrows pp24(t), 33,50(tl); Tim Davies
pp34, 76; Mark Duffin pp2, 29, 50(br), 52(b), 54, 74; Tony
Forbes/Sylvie Poggio pp3, 5, 6, 7(l), 65, 66; Peter Geisler/Specs
Art pp24(b), 42; Clive Goodyer/Pennant pp40, 41, 64; Tim
Kahane pp7(r), 21, 28, 32, 53; Terry McKenna/Linda Rogers
Associates pp8, 9, 13, 31, 71; Moondisks Limited p50(tr);
Julian Mosedale/Pennant pp30, 36, 52(t), 72; Sally Kindberg
pp22, 23, 35, 38; Pete Smith/Specs Art pp25, 26, 27; Simon
Turner/Specs Art pp43, 48, 57, 58, 59;
Planet icons by Mark Duffin
Cover design by Oliver Design
Cover illustration by Tim Kahane

The authors would like to thank Karen Spiller, Pilar García,
Claire Thacker, Angela Reckitt, Greg Sweetnam.

Sue Mohamed would like to thank Emma for her ideas and
ongoing encouragement.

Sagrario Salaberri would like to thank Felipe for his continuing
encouragement and support, and Sagrario, Alejandro and
Pablo Angel, without whom this book would certainly not
have been written.

Carmen Fernández Santás would like to thank Alvaro, Aida
and Daniel for their endless support and her students at I.E.S.
Antonio Fraguas for teaching her so much.

Liz Kilbey would like to thank Paul for trying out all the
exercises!

The publishers would like to thank Liz Kilbey for her
contribution to the project.

The authors and publishers would like to thank the following
for permission to reproduce their photographs:
Colorific p77(br); Eye Ubiquitous pp49,77(bl); Pictures
Colour Library pp56,77(tr); Redferns p14(t); REX p14(b);
Telegraph Colour Library p77(tl).

While every effort has been made to trace the owners of the
copyright material in this book, there have been some cases
when the publishers have been unable to contact the owners.
We should therefore be grateful to hear from anyone who
recognizes their copyright material and who is
unacknowledged. We shall be pleased to make the necessary
amendments in future editions of the book.

Printed and bound by Thomson Litho

2005
10 9 8 7 6 5 4